EASY WALKS TO LAKE DISTRICT VIEWS

MIKE PATEFIELD

© Mike Patefield, 2017

All Rights Reserved. No part of this publication may be reproduced, stored in a retrieval system, or transmitted in any form or by any means – electronic, mechanical, photocopying, recording, or otherwise – without prior written permission from the publisher or a licence permitting restricted copying issued by the Copyright Licensing Agency, 90 Tottenham Court Road, London W1P 0LA. This book may not be lent, resold, hired out or otherwise disposed of by trade in any form of binding or cover other than that in which it is published, without the prior consent of the publisher.

Moral Rights: The author has asserted his moral right to be identified as the Author of this Work.

Published by Sigma Leisure – an imprint of
Sigma Press, Stobart House, Pontyclerc, Penybanc Road, Ammanford, Carmarthenshire SA18 3HP.

British Library Cataloguing in Publication Data
A CIP record for this book is available from the British Library.

ISBN: 978-1-910758-33-5

Typesetting and Design by: Sigma Press, Ammanford.

Cover photograph: Wast Water (see page 30) – Britain's favourite view © Mike Patefield

Photographs: © Mike Patefield

Maps: Dr Rebecca Terry

Printed by: Akcent Media

Disclaimer: the information in this book is given in good faith and is believed to be correct at the time of publication. No responsibility is accepted by either the author or publisher for errors or omissions, or for any loss or injury however caused. Only you can judge your own fitness, competence and experience. Do not rely solely on sketch maps for navigation: we strongly recommend the use of appropriate Ordnance Survey (or equivalent) maps.

Dedicated to Jean Patefield
Writer of guide books
Who lived and walked in her beloved Lake District
1948-2016

Contents

		Distance (km/miles)	Height Gain (metres/feet)	OS map area	
Introduction					7
Area/Location Map					15

Very Easy

		Distance (km/miles)	Height Gain (metres/feet)	OS map area	
1.	Crummock Water *A lesser-known rival to Britain's favourite view*	2½/1½	10/30	NW	17
2.	Buttermere *Admire the sentinels*	7/4½	10/30	NW	21
3.	Claife Heights *A Victorian viewing station*	1½/1	30/100	SE	26
4.	Wasdale *Britain's favourite view*	6/4	30/100	SW	30
5.	Queen Adelaide's Hill *A gentle stroll with spectacular views*	1/¾	40/130	SE	36

Fairly Easy

6.	Rulbuts Hill *A peaceful rival to Orrest Head*	4½/3	45/150	SE	40
7.	Gummer's How *One of the best panoramic views of the Lake District*	2/1½	100/330	SE	45
8.	Sizergh and Helsington *Another panorama across the Lakes*	4½/3	110/360	SE	65
9.	Jenkin Crag *Views of Windermere*	4½/3	120/400	SE	72
10.	Orrest Head and Holehird *The view that inspired Alfred Wainwright*	6½/4	130/450	SE	78

	Distance (km/miles)	Height Gain (metres/feet)	OS map area	
11. **Heugh Scar and Heughscar Hill** *A ridge walk with views over Ullswater from the north*	4½/3	150/500	NE	84
12. **Brantwood and Coniston** *The café with the best views*	6½/4	150/500	SE	88

Not as Easy

	Distance	Height Gain	OS map	
13. **Castle Crag** *Views from the Jaws of Borrowdale*	5½/3½	210/700	NW	94
14. **Loughrigg Fell** *Outstanding views every step of the way round a Marilyn*	8/5	230/750	SE	99
15. **High Rigg** *Stunning views of Blencathra and Skiddaw*	9/5½	250/820	NE	106
16. **Black Crag** *Outstanding vistas at the heart of the southern Lake District*	9/5½	270/890	SE	113
17. **Oxford and Arnison Crags** *Two crags with views of Ullswater from the south*	4½/3	290/950	NE	119
18. **Lingmoor Fell** *Magnificent views of the Langdales*	5/3	290/950	SW	124
19. **Gowbarrow Fell and Ullswater** *The most beautiful lake*	7/4½	330/1100	NE	129
20. **Walla Crag and Friar's Crag** *One walk, three special viewpoints*	10/6½	350/1150	NW	137

Introduction

The Lake District is renowned for views of lakes and vistas of mountains and is England's best loved walking area. It has cast its spell over visitors since the earliest days of tourism over two hundred years ago. Crammed into this blessed corner of North West England is much that represents the best of British landscape. Deep U-shaped valleys dig into the landscape and stretch out into the distance, whilst rugged mountains soar skywards. The mountains are, in fact, modest in scale but by some trick of the eye, give every impression of brooding magnificence as they are mirrored in the serene lakes beneath. Tiny tarns lie like jewels among the hills just waiting to be discovered while between the hills are long dales of peaceful pasture with woods and rivers in which nestle ancient towns and delightful villages.

Thousands escape to its freedom and beauty every year and yet there are many quiet corners where its peace can be enjoyed away from the crowds. It exerts its special charm at all times of the year and is never the same as the light and weather change. No corner of England has attracted so many writers and artists and it has inspired some of the best loved poetry and prose.

It is my hope that this book will enable you to appreciate the Lake District and the wonders it has to offer through a range of diverse walks which all include exceptional views, some well-known and others that could be considered hidden gems. This introduction provides the back drop to this wonderful landscape, the history of which has moulded the breathtaking views and diverse landscape found on each walk.

To the visitor, the stretches of water and the mountains seem unchanging, their shapes as recognizable as the faces of well-loved friends. Taking a longer perspective, that is an illusion caused by our short life span compared with the immensity of geological time. At different periods in the Earth's history the area we know as one of mountains and lakes has been at the bottom of the sea, blasted by volcanos, an arid wind-blown desert and buried beneath thousands of feet of ice. All of these circumstances have contributed to the landscape we see today.

The Lakes today consists of three main types of rock surrounded by a rim of a fourth type. (Of course this statement is an oversimplification of what is a complex area geologically.) Each rock contributes its own distinctive landscape.

The oldest rocks are the Skiddaw slates in the north. They were formed from the mud and silt that accumulated on the bed of a vast ocean about 500 million years ago. Since then they have been covered by later deposits and uncovered and worn away by the erosive forces of water, wind and ice. They weather quite evenly and in doing so have produced the rounded, smooth hills such as Blencathra and Skiddaw, towering above Keswick.

The dramatic crags of central Lakeland such as Scafell and the Langdales originated in volcanoes which thrust through the sea bed with explosive violence, scattering fragments of rock far and wide. Lava flowed out and in periods of violent eruption, vast quantities of dust were ejected which later consolidated to form volcanic ash and breccia. The volcanic cones built up above the sea bed and again, vast layers of rock accumulated which are now known as the Borrowdale Volcanic series.

The third type of rock, Silurian slates, gives a comparatively gentle and pastoral landscape because it is more easily eroded and forms a deeper, more fertile soil. It is found in the south around Windermere and extends towards Kendal. It too was laid down at the bottom of the sea, from mud and silt particles formed from the erosion of ancient mountains.

Since these three categories of rock were formed the rock strata have been subject to stupendous physical forces: thrown up into folds by the colliding of continents and worn down by water, wind and ice. At one time, during the Carboniferous period some 300 million years ago, the land which is now the Lake District was covered by a warm, clear sea in which corals and other sea life flourished. Thick layers of limestone were formed. The sea was never very deep and eventually it filled up completely and was colonised by a marshy forest of huge ferns. From these the coal measures of the Whitehaven – Maryport coal field were formed and the fire clays under most of the seams are the remains of the soil in which this forest once grew. Eventually this limestone was eroded away and now remains as a rim around the Lake District.

The single most important influence forming the area we know today was ice. Over a million years ago the climate began to get colder and more snow fell than the sun could melt in the summer: the last great Ice Age had begun. Gradually it became thicker and thicker until only the tips of the highest mountains peeped through. Great glaciers ground their way down the valleys, carrying debris with them. Sometimes the climate became a bit warmer and the ice loosened its grip for a while only to re-advance and cover the land again.

The ice, loaded with rock debris, scoured the land. Valleys were deepened and straightened as jutting spurs were eroded. The shape of the valleys altered from the typical 'V' formed by water erosion to a more 'U' shape. Side valleys were left as hanging valleys by this deepening effect on the main valley. Rocks at the bottom of the valley were scratched by fragments of ice carried along by the glacier and these can still be seen today.

Some ten to twenty thousand years ago the ice began to melt, hopefully for the last time – though we have no assurance that there will not be a fresh advance: we may just be in a warm interglacial period, such as there has been before. As the ice melted masses of clay and debris were dumped and choked the natural outlets from the valleys. Thus many of the deepened valleys were dammed and the lakes were formed, fanning out like the spokes of a wheel from a central hub.

The lakes are the essential counterpoint to the mountains. The water which fills them and provides the music of the valleys as streams tumble over rocks was once rain. It is an inescapable fact of life that as moist air from the Atlantic rises to cross the land it cools and the water vapour condenses out and falls as rain. The Lake District does not have more rainy days than, say, London but Lake District rain can be prolonged and peculiarly wetting in its consistency. The wise walker goes prepared. Remember that William Wordsworth died of a cold caught, it is said, by walking in the rain without a hat!

The landscape we see today is not the product of geological forces and weather alone. Humanity may have visited the area before the last Ice Age but, if so, left no record. Since returning as the ice retreated, human beings have had as much impact on what we see as the ice did. Left to nature, all but the highest hills would be covered in a thick cloak of forest. Oak, mixed with other trees would cover the lower slopes and pine and birch scrub would grow on the higher hills, so only the top of the highest peaks would poke out above a sea of forest. Similarly the valleys such as Borrowdale, Langdale and Newlands would have been impassable with alder swamp. Over the centuries the landscape has been moulded to fit human purposes, so what we admire today is as much the creation of man as nature.

The transformation of the landscape began about five thousand years ago when human beings started to take control of the environment, almost unnoticeably at first but with ever increasing power, that led inexorably to the man-made landscape we see today. Not only could stone axes cut down the forest but animals such as pigs and goats grazing in the forest, nibbled away the young shoots and prevented the forest regenerating. Today there is virtually none of the original forest cover left, though the Keskadale oaks in the Newlands valley may be a remnant.

Much of the clearance of the primeval forest happened during the time after the Norman Conquest when the area was mainly dominated by the great abbeys such as Furness. The monks developed the wool trade by opening up the fells as sheep walks. As the soil was exposed it became impoverished due to the leaching of minerals by the rain and bracken and matt grass took over more and more. Animals which once roamed the Lake District such as boar, wolves and golden eagles, were driven from the land. The miles of dry stone walls, which now seem almost part of the natural landscape, were mainly built in the latter half of the eighteenth century and the first half of the nineteenth century, when labour was cheap. Population pressures drove farming into ever more remote and inaccessible areas.

The amount of woodland has increased due to reforestation and is now about ten percent. About half is native broadleaved woodland whilst the rest is conifer plantation. Five thousand acres of the broadleaved woodland is protected due to ownership by the National Trust and the Park Authority owns over a thousand acres more. Some of the woods are Sites of Special Scientific Interest because of their lichens, mosses and liverworts. The woods still harbour red squirrels and are home to many red deer, a rare sight for noisy human visitors.

Teals, tufted ducks, merganser, goosander, mallard and mute swans breed in the Lakes and are joined in winter by many visitors such as goldeneye and widgeon. Ravens and peregrine falcons swoop over the fells and crags and a native bird, the golden eagle, returned but may well have died.

Though today we do not think of it as such, the area has long been an industrial area. The value of the volcanic stone in the centre of the Lake District was recognised five thousand years ago and used to make stone axes, which were exported to Ireland and Brittany as well as other parts of Britain. Another valuable product torn from the heart of the area is slate. It was used by the Romans to roof their buildings and is still quarried today. Unlike more fertile areas, the Romans seem to have come to the Lakes more as an army of occupation than to settle. They were attracted by the copper and lead in the rocks and the mining of these metals has been an important local industry until quite recent times. In the reign of Queen Elizabeth I, German miners were brought to the Lake District to improve the efficiency of mining. The Moot Hall in Keswick was rebuilt in 1571 as the Queen's receiving house for copper. Smelting was carried out at Brigham by the river Greta and the works were considered the finest of their kind in Europe in their day.

The beauty and grandeur of the Lake District has inspired generations of artists and writers. William Wordsworth was the quintessential poet of place and several of the walks in this book visit the localities associated with him. He attracted many leading literary contemporaries to the Lakes, most notably Samuel Taylor Coleridge and Robert Southey. The friends and colleagues who visited Wordsworth were the vanguard of the army of tourists, who have been drawn to the region since the eighteenth century. Wordsworth wrote his famous *Guide to the Lakes* but regretted the invasion of tourists and campaigned against the coming of the railway which opened up the area to the less leisured and less wealthy (though he apparently owned shares in the railway company).

Wordsworth wrote his guide in 1835 but he was not the first and has been followed by countless others. One of the most interesting was Harriet Martineau whose *Complete Guide to the English Lakes* was published in 1855. It is a racy and idiosyncratic mixture of fact, legend, hearsay and political comment. She was born in Norwich in 1802 and was plain, almost deaf and subject to periods of ill health. Not surprisingly, she did not have the sweetest of tempers. When her father died in 1825 she had to make a living in a world where education and opportunities for women were severely restricted. She achieved this with her needle and her pen and achieved success as a journalist and commentator. In 1846 she had a house built near Ambleside and was visited by many Establishment figures of the day, despite her stern manner and Radical views.

Not all the writers inspired by the Lake District have been moved to great poetry. Arthur Ransome based his children's classics, of which *Swallows and Amazons* is the most famous, in the Lakeland. Beatrix Potter was inspired by family holidays in the Lakes and later moved here, married and as Mrs William

Heelis took up sheep farming. She used the money she made to buy tracts of land which she gave to the National Trust.

The author who has done most to present Lakeland to a wide audience is Alfred Wainwright. He was born in Blackburn in 1907 and worked in local government. He fell in love with the area during walking trips as a young man and in 1941 he moved to Kendal where he eventually became Borough Treasurer. His seven *Pictorial Guides to the Lakeland Fells* were compiled between 1952 and 1966 and his evocative descriptions, distinctive drawings and acerbic asides have made them the indispensable companion of all fell walkers.

The Lake District is so small and vulnerable that it could easily be loved to death. Some sort of protection and management is vital to conserve what Wordsworth referred to as 'a sort of national property'. Two important, though very different, bodies are the National Trust and the National Park.

The National Trust was founded by three Victorians of energy and enthusiasm. One was Canon Harwicke Rawnsley, who was the vicar of Crosthwaite near Keswick as well as being a poet, athlete, traveller and historian. A parishioner told him in 1890 that he had been forced to buy a piece of land from a neighbour to prevent some fine trees being felled. Rawnsley took the idea of protection by purchase and, with Octavia Hill and Robert Hunter, the National Trust was launched in 1895. It aims to acquire land and property of scenic beauty or historical interest and under the National Trust Act of 1907 it can declare its property 'inalienable'. This means that it cannot be sold or mortgaged and later legislation gave it the right to appeal to Parliament against compulsory purchase orders.

Today the National Trust – which is not a government department or quango but a charity depending on its millions of members for support – is the largest landowner in the Lake District. Much of its property was acquired by gift. For example, Beatrix Potter gave 4,000 acres including fourteen farms. The work of the National Trust has enabled traditional farming practices to continue and so conserved the well-loved landscape. One advantage of the National Trust from the point of view of the visitor is that its properties are open to the public, subject only to the needs of farming, forestry and the conservation of wildlife.

The first National Park in the world was Yellowstone in the USA, created in 1872 to protect that magnificent area of wilderness from development. In

England, by the time the idea caught on, there was no wilderness left. Thus, in an English context, the term National Parks is something of a misnomer since they are neither National nor parks! Unlike the USA for example, the land is not owned by the nation but by private individuals or bodies such as the National Trust, and within the bounds are towns and villages. Agriculture and industry continue. It is more of a planning concept to give special protection to areas of outstanding landscape value.

The Lake District is the largest of the National Parks in England and Wales and the Act, delayed by the War, which brought them into being was passed in 1949, seventy-seven years after the establishment of Yellowstone. The National Park Authority has planning control, provides information and ranger services and also maintains footpaths. In addition it owns tracts of common land, woods and some of the lakes. The National Park works closely with the National Trust and other large landowners, to provide a degree of protection and public access unrivalled elsewhere in England.

The walks

The twenty walks in this book are all between 1½ and 6½ miles and should be within the capacity of the average person. They are intended to take the walker to some of the loveliest scenery viewpoints in England at a gentle pace. To fully appreciate the countryside it is necessary to go slowly with your eyes and ears open.

The walks are ordered from very easy ones which are almost level, with views of the lakes and surrounding mountains, to others which explore the lower fells and so involve some climbing. From these there are outstanding views of the highest mountains. The contents list includes both an approximate length of the walk and the height gained – the total uphill walking. Even the last walk is easy compared with climbing the high mountains such as Scafell Pike and Great Gable. Hence, you will be able to choose a walk suitable for the day. Uphill walking presents no problem to the sensible walker who has three gears – slowly, very slowly and admiring the view. None of the walks in this book are inherently hazardous but sensible care should be taken. A lot of the falls which do happen are due to unsuitable footwear, particularly smooth soles, since steep grass can be as slippery as can the more obviously hazardous wet, smooth rock. Proper walking shoes or boots also give some protection to the ankle. It is also essential to look where you are putting your feet to avoid tripping up. Wainwright said that he never had a serious fall in all his years and thousands of miles of walking because he always looked where he put his feet and he stopped if he wanted to admire the scenery.

All the routes are on public rights of way, permissive paths or open fell and have been carefully checked but, of course, in the countryside things do change; a gate is replaced by a stile or a wood is extended. In the Lake District the paths are often (but not always) well used and well maintained so the routes are easy to follow.

Each walk is illustrated by a map and all except the ones to Views 3 and 7 are circular. An Ordnance Survey map is useful as well, especially for identifying the main features of views. The Lake District is covered by four widely available Explorer 1:25000 (2½ inches to 1 mile) maps in the Outdoor Leisure Series. OL4 covers the north-western area, OL5 the north-eastern area, OL6 the south-western area and OL7 the south-eastern area. The contents list indicates the map covering each walk.

A number of walks can be reached using the local bus service. Timetables are posted on some bus stops and are available on the buses, at tourist information centres or on the website **www.stagecoachbus.com**. The walks start at places where a car may be left, usually a public car park, and alternative starting places are mentioned for if these are convenient.

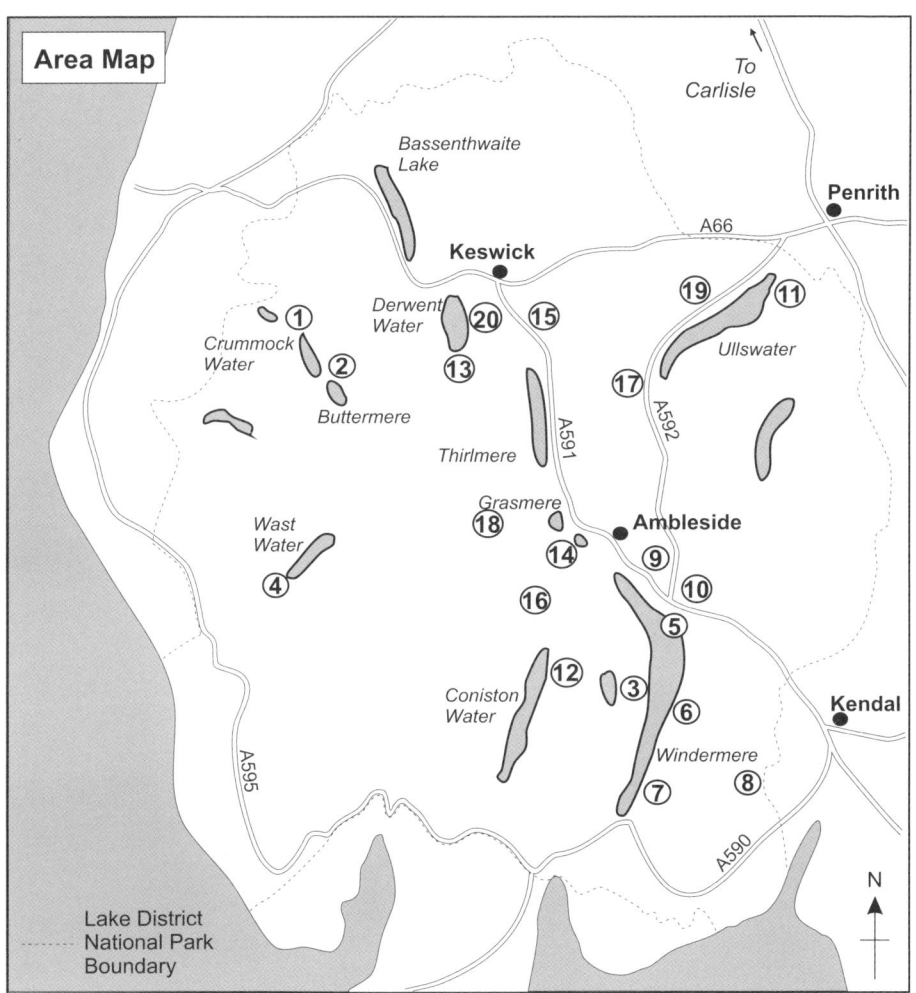

View 1: Crummock Water
A lesser-known rival to Britain's favourite view

This is short and easy level walk that wends its way to the shore of Crummock Water for a stroll by the lake. Crummock Water is often overlooked by its sister lake Buttermere (see View 2). The route to and from the lake is a pleasing combination of woods and quiet field paths and tracks. On the outward leg there are superb views into the central fells including a view down Crummock Water that rivals, if not surpasses, Britain's Favourite View which appears on the front cover (see View 4).

What you need to know	
Walking distance	2½km/1½ miles; Height gain: 10m/30 feet
Map	OS Explorer OL4 The English Lakes North-western area
Starting point	Lanthwaite Wood. Grid reference: NY149215
How to get there	From the B5289, Buttermere Cockermouth road, follow the signs to Loweswater, along the C2030, to a National Trust car park (free to members) on the left after about one mile. This is immediately before a bridge over the river Cocker
Refreshments	None on the route but the Kirkstile Inn in nearby Loweswater village is a wonderful old pub housed in buildings that date back to the 16th century and serves excellent food

Walk Directions

1. From the entrance to the car park walk along the track signed 'Lanthwaite 1 mile', passing to the left of the car park. At the end of the car park, go

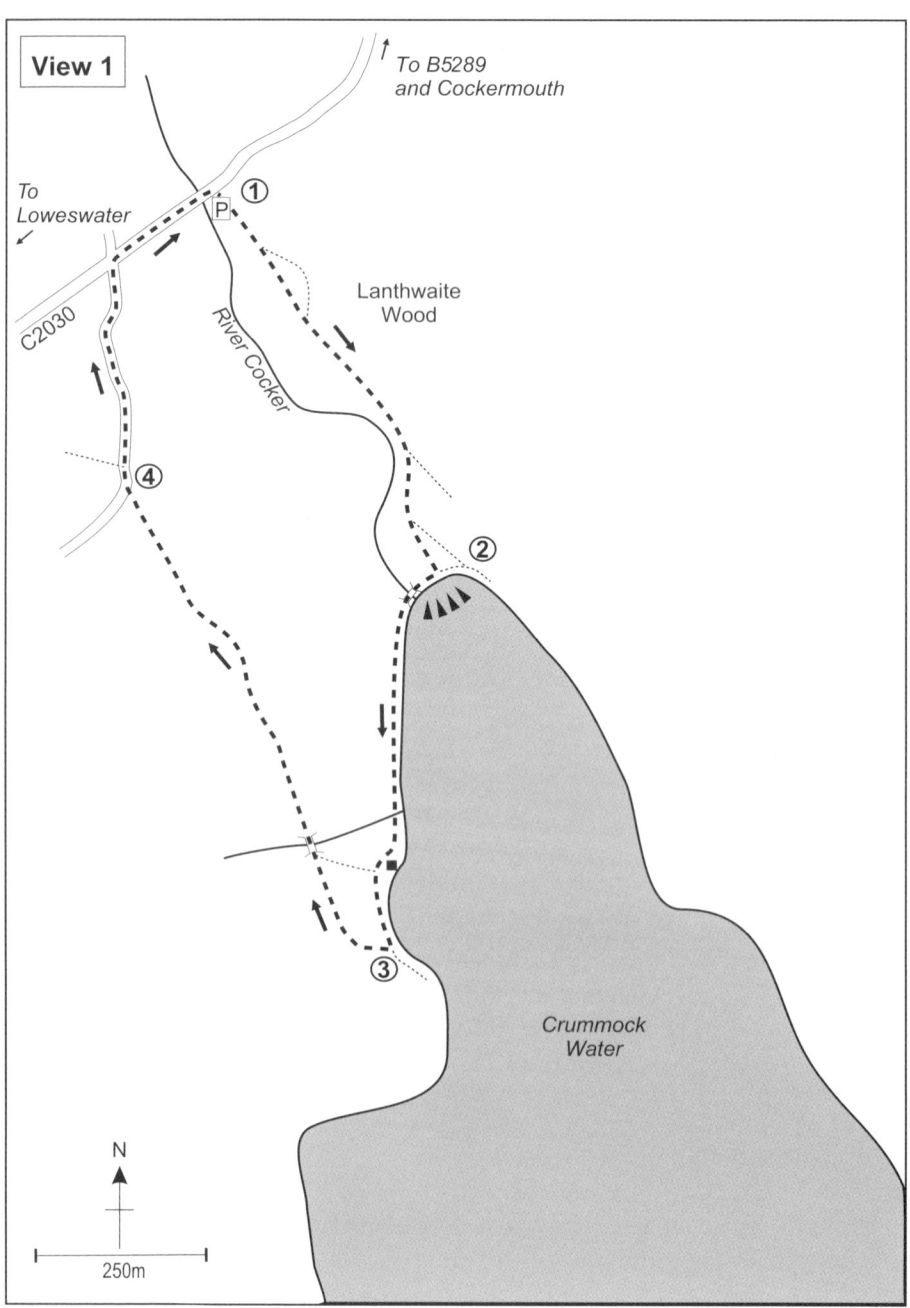

through a gate and continue along the track. Bear right at a fork. Keep ahead as a path joins on the left and then bear right again at two more forks to reach a shingle beach at Crummock Water, with a seat to admire the magnificent view down the lake. See plate 1, page 49.

The view down Crummock Water encompasses the fells of Mellbreak and Red Pike to the right of the lake. Grassmoor and Rannerdale Knotts are to the left.

The lake is 2½ miles long of clear water. The level was raised by three feet at the start of the 20th century by building a weir, which incorporates a fish ladder, and can still be seen today. This was done to improve the water supply to Workington and the plaque on the pump house, passed a little further on, reflects the civic pride by Workington Corporation in the achievement. The plaque is on the side facing you as you approach the pump house. The water is supplied to the towns of Whitehaven, Workington, Maryport and Silloth and many villages.

2. Turn right to walk by the lake, crossing the river Cocker at a couple of footbridges and past the fish weir and pump house. Continue by the lake, alongside a concrete barrier, to a kissing gate.

    The river Cocker, which drains Crummock Water, usually appears peaceful. It flows into the river Derwent at Cockermouth. Perhaps not surprisingly, the town is prone to flooding and you may recall the devastating inundations of November 2009 and December 2015 from which the community has made a spirited recovery. This charming small town has something to interest everyone and it is an enjoyable place to just wander, with many unique specialist shops.

3. Immediately after the gate turn right along the right hand side of a field and after 50 yards go through a gate on the right. Continue along a walkway, over a stile and ahead to a bridge. Over the bridge continue on a fenced and gated track to a lane.

4. Turn right to a crossroads and then turn right again to walk along the C2030 to the far side of the bridge over the river Cocker where this walk started.

River Cocker

C roads are rarely labelled on signposts or marked on Ordnance Survey Explorer maps. The National Street Gazetteer is the definitive reference dataset of streets within England and Wales but is neither public data nor open data.

The C2030 leads to Loweswater village and on to the lake with the same name; well away from the much more crowded parts of the Lake District. There is an excellent short walk round the lake starting at either the National Trust car park at Maggie's Bridge at the south-east end of the lake or on the roadside at Waterend at the north-west end of the lake.

View 2: Buttermere
Admire the sentinels

Buttermere has long been recognised as perhaps the most perfect of Lakeland's smaller lakes and its circumnavigation is a well-deserved popular walk. There are outstanding views of the surrounding fells all the way round the lake, ideal if you wish to see the mountains without any climbing. Halfway round the lake, you pass the 'Sentinels', the Lake District's most photographed trees.

What you need to know	
Walking distance	7 km. 4½ miles. Height gain: 10 m. 30 feet
Map	OS Explorer OL4 The English Lakes North-western area
Starting point	The Bridge Hotel, Buttermere. Grid reference: NY174169
How to get there	Buttermere village is on the B5289 Borrowdale Cockermouth road and may also be reached from the A66 at Braithwaite via the beautiful Newlands valley. The Bridge Hotel is on the B5289. There is a National Park pay-and-display car park in the village and a National Trust car park (charge for non-members) about ¼ mile north of the village or some parking beside the Newlands road, signed 'Keswick 8½' just past the church. The seasonal 77 and 77A buses from Keswick also serve Buttermere
Alternative starting point	Gatesgarth Farm pay-and-display car park on the B5289 about 2 miles south-east of Buttermere village. Grid reference: NY195149. You would then start the walk at point 5, or to just admire the view of the sentinels walk along the road as far as the lakeshore

Refreshments	There is plenty of choice including Syke Farm Tearoom near the start of the walk, the Fish Inn and Croft House Farm Café near the end

Walk Directions

On the Borrowdale road at the junction with the Newlands road is the small and beautiful Church of St. James where sixteen angels look down from where the roofing timbers meet the wall. Note also the shepherd and his sheep forming part of the metal entrance gate.

Church of St. James

1. With your back to the Bridge Hotel, follow the road to your right in the direction of Borrowdale for 70 yards. Bear right on a path through Syke

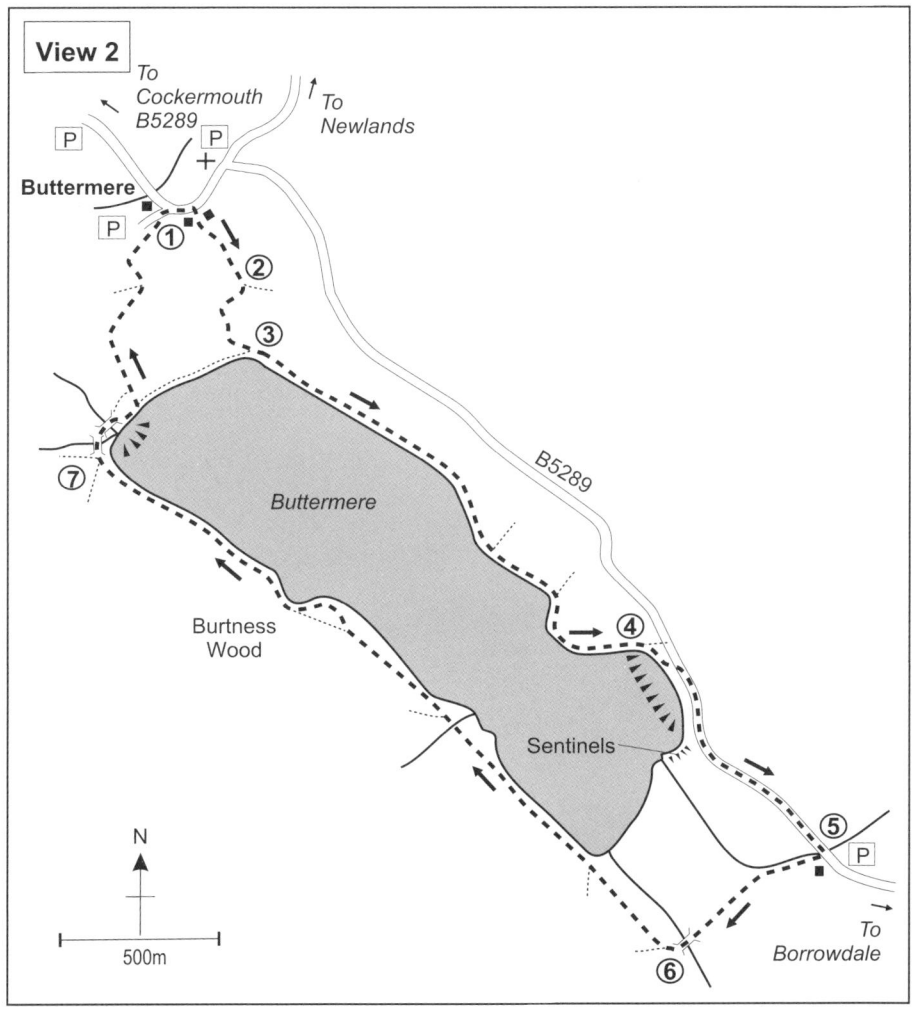

Farm yard signed 'Lakeshore Path'. Go along the track between farm buildings to a small gate on the right.

2. Turn right through the gate signed 'Shoreline Path' and follow the initially fenced path to the lake.

3. At the lake, continue ahead on a wooded path with the lake on your right. Go through a tunnel and continue along the lakeshore path. This soon becomes a track.

   As you approach the end of the lake, you reach the classic view (see plate 2, page 49) of the Sentinels, the row of scots pine trees dominated by Fleetwith Pike and Haystacks beyond. If you are lucky enough to be here when the lake is calm and the sun is low, you will never forget the stunning reflection of the Sentinels and fells in the lake over which they preside.

4. When the track goes up to a road, bear right on the lakeshore path. This soon joins the road. Walk along the road for about ½ mile.

   As you continue around the lake, as well as Haystacks, the backdrop to the trees incorporates High Crag, one of the fells that is part of the High Stile range above the far shore of Buttermere.

5. At Gatesgarth Farm turn right on a public bridleway signed 'Buttermere Ennerdale'.

6. When level with the far side of the lake, go through a gate and turn right. Stay on the lakeshore path and enter a wood. At a junction bear right to regain the lakeshore.

   As you cross Comb Beck at a footbridge look left to see the waterfalls plunging down from High Stile. These are particularly impressive after heavy rain.

7. At the end of the lake, turn right through a gate and over a footbridge and then over a larger footbridge. Turn right to the lakeshore for an impressive view down the length of Buttermere (plate 3, page 50). Walk to the end of the field and turn left. Go through a gate and follow the track back to Buttermere village.

   Buttermere and Crummock Water were once one lake, lying in a U-shaped glacial valley running north-west from the jagged peaks of Fleetwith Pike and Haystacks. The two lakes occupy most of the valley with the village of

Buttermere in between; the name possibly coming from butter lake, the lake with good pasture.

Gatesgarth Farm is important for its Herdwick sheep. It is one of a number of fell-going flocks in the Buttermere Valley where in addition to Herdwick flocks there are also Swaledale and Rough Fell flocks.

Turner visited Buttermere in 1797, early in his career and produced the painting entitled 'Buttermere Lake, with Part of Cromackwater, Cumberland, a Shower'. The view is from the southern end of Crummock Water and shows a glimpse of Buttermere.

To visit the shore of Crummock Water go towards the end of the National Park car park and through a small gate on the right to follow the path beside the river, Mill Beck. Do not go across the footbridge. Continue past another footbridge then bear slightly left to stay by the beck. Follow the path over the shoulder of a wooded knoll to the shore of Crummock Water.

Crummock Water from the south-eastern shore with the snow on Mellbreak merging into the leaden sky

View 3: Claife Heights
A Victorian viewing station

At Claife Heights, is Claife Viewing Station, built in the 1790s for visitors to view Lake Windermere. It was most fashionable with tourists in the earlier part of the 19th century. There are many ways of getting there. The walk described here starts on the eastern shore of the lake and incorporates a very short cruise on the lake.

What you need to know	
Walking distance	1½ km. 1 mile Height gain: 30 m. 100 feet
Map	OS Explorer OL7 The English Lakes South-eastern area
Starting point	Ferry Nab car park Bowness (charge). Grid reference: SD398959
How to get there	From the A592 about ½ mile south of Bowness, take the B5285 signed 'Hawkshead Coniston via Ferry' to the car park on the right. Bowness can be reached by the 599 bus service
Alternative starting point	Ash Landing National Trust car park (charge for non-members) on the B5285. From the Hawkshead direction this car park is on the left at a right hand bend shortly after reaching the lakeshore. From the ferry it is on the right at a left hand bend
Refreshments	The Courtyard Café is passed on the way from the ferry to the viewing station

Walk Directions

1. From Ferry Nab car park, return to the road and turn right to the ferry. Catch the car ferry across the lake. It runs every 20 minutes and costs 50p for passengers at the time of writing.

   The Windermere Ferry has been operating for more than 500 years. The original craft were rowed across the lake, later ferries were steam driven and current ferry 'Mallard' has diesel engines and runs along visible underwater blue cables.

The Windermere Ferry

2. When you disembark, take the road ahead for 130 yards. Turn right on a path signed 'Claife Viewing Station ¼ mile'. Follow the lakeshore to a lane.

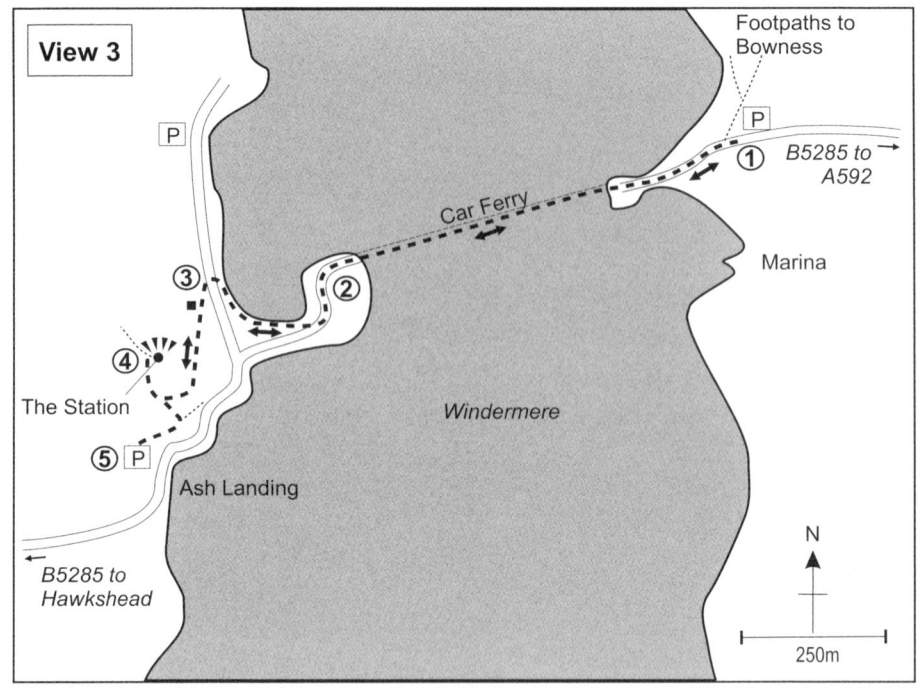

On the left of the road are the Freshwater Biological Association buildings. They aim to promote freshwater biology and the sound and sustainable management of freshwater systems.

3. Turn left signed 'Claife Viewing Station ¼ mile' and immediately bear right into the courtyard with the café on the right and outdoor seating on the left. Continue up to Claife Viewing Station. In the building go up the spiral staircase to the remains of the drawing room with coloured glass outlining the views (see plate 4, page 50). Listen to the Aeolian Harp.

Visitors haven't always flocked to the Lake District for holidays. Until the start of the Picturesque Movement in the 1700s, the Lake District was thought to be an unattractive wilderness – certainly not a place for tourists. However, by the late 18th century people set out to 'view' the landscape in a pre-determined way. The viewing station was built in the 1790s and enlarged in 1801 to include a dining room and wine cellar on the ground floor. The drawing room on the first floor is reached by a spiral staircase and had windows tinted with coloured glass, designed to recreate the landscape under different seasonal conditions. Yellow created a summer landscape, orange an autumn one, light green for spring, light blue for winter, dark blue for moonlight and lilac to give the impression of a thunderstorm. In the 1830s and 1840s it was used by wealthy visitors for parties and dances. This quote from Mary Maria Higginson, who attended a dinner dance at Claife Viewing Station in the nineteenth century, paints a vivid picture of what it was like to come here: "The very nicest dance that I can call to mind was given by a friend at a place called The Station. It was built on account of the beautiful view it commanded, both up and down Windermere ... the winding walks around the Station lighted up with Chinese lanterns and coloured lamps made charming promenades."

By the end of the 19th century Claife Viewing Station had fallen out of favour and fell into disrepair. The remains have recently been re-opened by the National Trust so you can imagine what these views might have been like.

4. Return the same way.

   OR

5. From Ash Landing car park, with your back to the lake, take a path in the far right hand corner signed 'Claife Viewing Station ¼ mile Station Cottage & Courtyard ½ mile Ferry ¾ mile' and then take the steps on the left signed 'Claife Viewing Station 100 yards Ferry ½ mile' up to the Viewing Station. Some of the distances are clearly less than those signed.

VIEW 4: WASDALE
BRITAIN'S FAVOURITE VIEW

Wast Water is one of the more remote lakes in the National Park and is very distinctive. Towering over the southern shore are the Wasdale screes, a steep fellside crumbling into the dark water beneath. The sheet of water leads to a backdrop of some of the most majestic fells such as Scafell and Great Gable and the prospect from the end of the lake was voted Britain's Favourite View in the TV programme of the same name in 2005. Comparatively few people enjoy it because you have to walk there – and that is where this route goes. Choose a clear and sunny day (Wast Water is definitely not at its scenic best in Lakeland drizzle), preferably with a dusting of snow on the tops and I guarantee you will not be disappointed – and don't forget your camera!

What you need to know	
Walking distance	6 km. 4 miles. Height gain: 30 m. 100 feet
Map	OS Explorer OL6 The English Lakes South-western area
Starting point	Cinderdale Bridge. Grid reference: NY128038
How to get there	From the A595 Barrow Whitehaven road, 2½ miles north of Ravenglass, take a minor road east signed 'Wasdale Head 9 Santon Bridge 2½'. After 1½ miles continue signed 'Santon Bridge 1 Wasdale 3¼' for a mile to a T-junction. Turn left signed 'Wasdale 2½ Gosforth 3 Whitehaven 15'. After about 200 yards turn right signed signed 'Wasdale 2½ Gosforth 3 Whitehaven 15'. After a further 2 miles cross a bridge over the river Irt and continue to a signed car park on the left after 50 yards
Alternative starting point	For a short walk of about one mile, there is a very limited amount of roadside parking on the Wasdale

Alternative starting point Cont'd	Head road just before it reaches the lake at point 6, Grid Reference: NY148048. Take the lakeshore path at point 6 to the viewpoint at the end of the lake and return the same way
Refreshments	None on the route but the Strands Hotel, Nether Wasdale is only about ½ mile to the north-west of Cinderdale Bridge

Walk Directions

1. Return to the road and turn right over a bridge, ignoring a lane on the left.

2. Some 30 yards after crossing the bridge, take the first public footpath on the left signed 'Wastwater' along the track to Easthwaite Farm.

   As you walk along the track, you see the Wasdale screes in all their glory with Kirk Fell and Great Gable peeking out to their left (see plate 5, page 51).

3. Just before entering the farmyard, take a permitted path on the left avoiding the farmyard. This follows a track passing to the left of farm buildings and after going through two gates joins the track from the farm. Turn left and continue through two more gates.

4. At a right hand bend immediately after passing through the second gate, turn left off the track on an unmarked path along the left hand side of a field to a river. This path is not at all obvious, at the time of writing, as previous way-marking has disappeared. At the river turn left on a riverside path for 25 yards to a bridge over the river.

5. Cross the bridge over the river Irt. Go ahead for 20 yards and through a kissing gate ahead to a fork after a few yards. Bear right and follow the path through the woods, ignoring a path on the left, to reach a boathouse where the river leaves the lake. Carry on beside the lake, soon reaching the classic viewpoint up the lake with the screes looming over it and the

panorama of fells beyond the head of the valley dominated by the towering Great Gable. There are seats well-placed to admire it. The view is on the front cover. The path continues beside the lake with Wasdale Hall youth hostel to the left and the magnificence of the screes on the other side of the lake. Eventually the lakeside path goes up steps to a ladder stile then climbs up to a lane.

The great fans of scree that tumble down into Wast Water are an awesome sight. When the lake was gouged out by a glacier during the last Ice Age, the southern slope was undercut and has been at the unstable angle of about 35° ever since the ice retreated 12,000 years ago. Occasionally a huge mass thunders down but some of the massive boulders, apparently perched precariously, are known to have been in the same spot for many years. The scree slopes are about 1,700 feet high and extend to the bottom of the lake, 258 feet below the surface. There is said to be a gnome garden complete with picket fence at the bottom of Wast Water. It was apparently

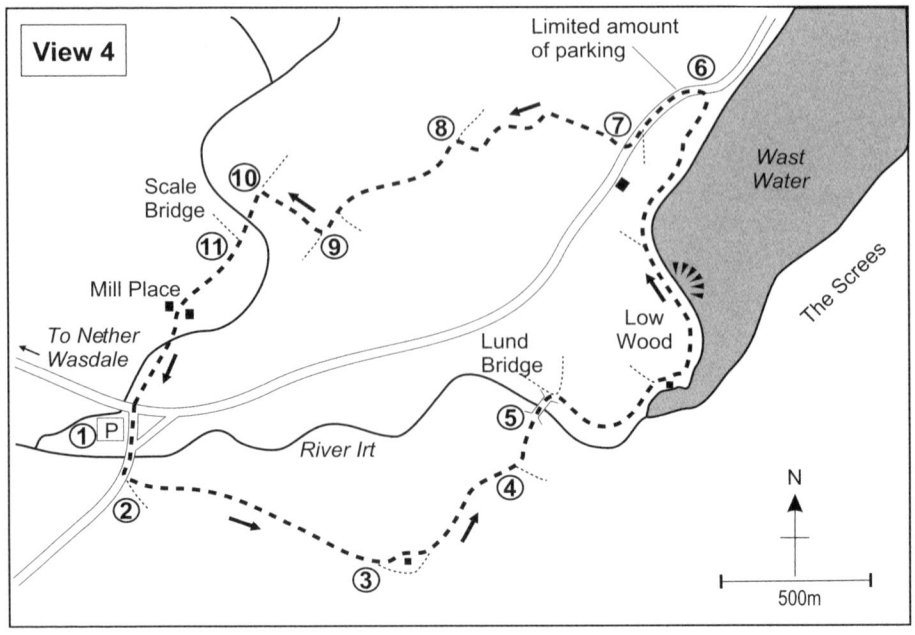

The Wasdale Screes

removed by police divers at the behest of the National Park Authority after some divers died after spending too long, too deep searching for the little fellows. However, the rumour is that it has been replaced at a greater depth, beyond that to which the police are allowed to dive by their elf and safety rules.

6. Turn left along the lane for about 300 yards.

7. About 20 yards after a kissing gate on the left, turn right on an unsigned path along a track to a gate. (There used to be a sign on the post to the right of the track but this has disappeared). Pass the walled enclosure on the right, which was the kitchen garden of Wasdale Hall. At the end of the wall continue ahead to a ladder stile by a gate. Through the gate, carry on along the path as it bears left and wends its way across a possibly boggy moss to a T-junction with a cross path.

Wasdale Hall is 200 years old and was originally used as a lakeside holiday home before becoming a National Trust property and youth hostel. It still retains many of its original features including paneled windows, gabled roof and cornicing.

8. Turn left and follow the well-defined path through a gate after which the path is enclosed by wire fences.

9. Immediately after another gate, turn right on a similarly enclosed path signed 'Scale Bridge 130 yards' to reach two gateways. Continue through the one on the right to a T-junction with a bridleway in front of a fence.

10. Turn left signed 'Cinderdale Bridge ½ mile'. Go over Scale Bridge across a stream then walk across a field to a gate. (Note that the distance to the bridge is well over the 130 yards previously signed.)

11. Immediately through the gate turn left signed 'Cinderdale Bridge ½ mile'. Walk with a wall on your left to farm buildings at Mill Place and continue on a track to a road. Cross the road and go ahead back to where this walk started.

For further magnificent views of Wasdale, drive along the minor road from Nether Wasdale beside the lake, crossed at point 6 on the walk, to Wasdale Head. Wasdale is a place that invites superlatives: not only England's highest mountain (Scafell) and deepest lake but also England's smallest church (though this is disputed) and once home to England's biggest liar.

St Olaf's in Wasdale Head is a tiny church that seats just 39 people. The building itself is of unknown date, though probably Tudor, and the roof beams are said to come from a Viking longboat. It was upgraded in 1892 to look like it does today; prior to this date the records show the building had an earthen floor, few or no seats, a hurdle at the doorway and no glass in the windows, hence the steeply sloping window sills that were an attempt to keep the rain out. The mountains are not always safe and in the churchyard are the graves of many climbers who died on the surrounding fells. The south window has a stained glass image of Napes Needle and the quotation 'I will lift up mine eyes unto the hills from whence cometh my strength'. The window is a memorial to members of the Fell & Rock Climbing Club who gave their lives in the First World War.

The greatest liar was 19th century publican Will Ritson, who loved to regale his customers with whoppers. For example, he claimed that Wasdale turnips are so big they could be used as sheds once Sunday lunch had been quarried out of them. An annual greatest liar competition is held in November at the Bridge Inn in Santon Bridge in his honour to award the title of "The Biggest Liar in the World" to the person who is worthy of following in the footsteps of "Auld Will". The contest attracts world-wide attention, and in recent years the audience has learned facts like how the Lake District was formed – not by ice or volcanic action, but by large moles and eels!

View 5: Queen Adelaide's Hill
A gentle stroll with spectacular views

The route first climbs a low hill (this is the Lake District after all!) for truly outstanding views of Windermere with the iconic Langdales beyond. The hill was originally called Rayrigg Bank and was renamed after a visit in 1840 by the Dowager Queen Adelaide, widow of William IV and aunt of Queen Victoria. There used to be a plaque marking the spot where she landed. It is a drumlin, a heap of stones picked up by a glacier and dropped when it melted at the end of the Ice Age. As you go over the hill, more views of the southern end of the lake open up before you. The route then leads along the tree-lined lakeshore, passing a once popular bathing spot (you could have a swim if you are so inclined) and an ancient ferryman's cottage before returning over an old stone bridge and beside the tumbling waters of Wynlass Beck.

What you need to know	
Walking distance	1 km. ¾ mile Height gain: 40 m. 130 feet
Map	OS Explorer OL7 The English Lakes South-eastern area
Starting point	Lay-by at Millerground. Grid reference: SD404987
How to get there	From the junction of the A591 and A592 near Windermere take the A592 signed 'Bowness Bay & the Lake Newby Bridge' for about ½ mile. Go past the Hammerbank car park to a lay-by on the right about a mile north of Bowness
Alternative starting point	Rayrigg Meadow car park (charge) a further ¼ mile south on the A592. You will then start the walk at point 3
Refreshments	None. A wide choice in Bowness

Walk Directions

1. Go through the gate at the southern end of the lay-by and take the path ahead. As you ascend extensive views of Windermere (lake) come into view. There is a bench seat near the highest point to take in the hill-top view over the lake to the fells beyond. See plate 6, page 51.

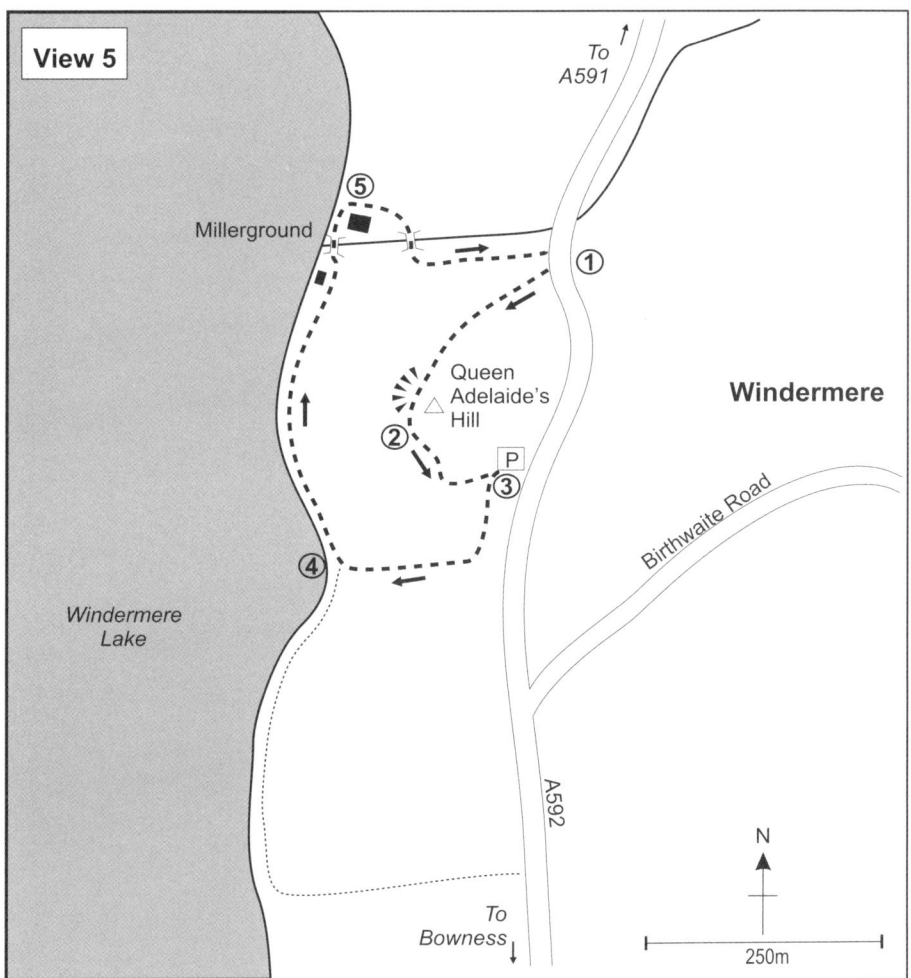

Wynlass Beck

2. At the second bench seat turn left to take a gravel path down to a car park.

3. Cross the corner of the car park to take a path on the right signed 'Lakeshore Footpath Picnic Area' onto Rayrigg Meadow where there is an information board with pictures of the flora and fauna you might see. Follow the path down to the lakeshore where there are two jetties.

   The building you see on your left near the road is the Windermere Outdoor Adventure Centre who specialise in all things water, including canoeing, kayaking, windsurfing and sailing. **www.better.org.uk/leisure-centre/south-lakeland/windermere**

   Most of the time it is difficult to imagine how different the water level can be after heavy rainfall. Not only are the jetties covered but the water may rise several feet higher still.

4. Turn right along the tree lined lakeshore path. Go through a gate to pass to the right of the Windermere Sea Scouts hut and then through a kissing gate on the left to continue across a beck.

   This is Low Millerground where there is a well positioned seat to take in the view of the lake and fells from the lakeshore. The Sea Scout huts started life as the changing rooms for outdoor swimming. Perhaps we are not as hardy as people were then and it fell into disuse when an indoor pool opened at Troutbeck Bridge. In those days, before the weir at Newby Bridge was built, the lake levels were often lower than they are today.

   Millerground Cottage is a Grade II Listed building, thought to date from the early 17th century. If you look at the end facing the lake you will see there is a small open tower on the roof. This held the bell to summon the ferry across the lake, though there is scant hard evidence that such a ferry ever existed. At the rear of the building there is a small round Westmorland chimney; larger ones are encountered in View 8.

5. Turn right to pass to the left of Millerground Cottage. Re-cross the beck at an old stone bridge and follow the path up beside the pretty cascades of Wynlass Beck back to the start.

View 6: Rulbuts Hill
A peaceful rival to Orrest Head

This short walk takes you with relatively little ascent to two viewpoints high above the east side of Windermere (lake). There are some excellent views, especially on the outward leg, and the highlight is the 360° panorama from Rulbuts Hill. At 175 metres (574 feet) high it is insignificant among the Lake District hills (and overlooked by Wainwright) but the views rival those from many loftier peaks. The paths can be muddy after heavy rain.

What you need to know	
Walking distance	4½ km. 3 miles. Height gain: 45 m. 150 feet
Map	OS Explorer OL7 The English Lakes South-eastern area
Starting point	Ghyll Head reservoir. Grid reference: SD398924
How to get there	From the A592, Bowness Newby Bridge road, about 2½ miles south of Bowness take a minor road east, signed 'Cartmell Fell Fell Road only' and 'Ghyll Head'. Drive along the lane for about ½ mile to an informal parking area with two large gates on the left. Note: Do not be misled by a small parking area also on the left but with no gates, before you arrive at the correct starting point
Refreshments	A wide choice in Bowness or at Fell Foot Park about 4 miles south on the A592

Walk Directions

Visible over the wall across the road from the starting place is the very attractive Ghyll Head tarn. This is entirely artificial and was originally built to provide a water supply for the Windermere area. It is now only needed when supplies are low and is managed as a very popular fishery. It is on private land, access being exclusively for members of the Windermere Fishing Association, who regularly stock it with trout.

1. Go through the high kissing gate next to the gate on the right and follow the path ahead signed 'Black Beck & Rosthwaite'. Ignore a path bearing right after 50 yards and go through a second gate. Keep on this path beside a fence and along a raised walkway to another high gate into woodland. At the end of the wood the path is less clear but bear slightly left to a waymark post to the right of a tree to reach a T-junction with a wide path. Go ahead, slightly left, on a faint path up onto Rosthwaite Heights where you will find a wonderfully positioned seat next to a cairn.

   The seat is inscribed 'Richard's Favourite Spot' and the view up the lake to the fells beyond, rivals that from Rulbut's Hill. Grizedale Forest is straight across the lake with the Coniston range beyond. See plate 7, page 52.

Richard's Favourite Spot

2. Return to the finger post and now turn left, signed 'Rosthwaite'. Cross two small streams, using stepping stones. Continue over a stile beside a gate, and then through a further gate to an attractive collection of buildings facing a small tarn. Carry on, now on a drive, to the end of the buildings and tarn.

Note the statuary, swans by the tarn and a magnificent horse ahead.

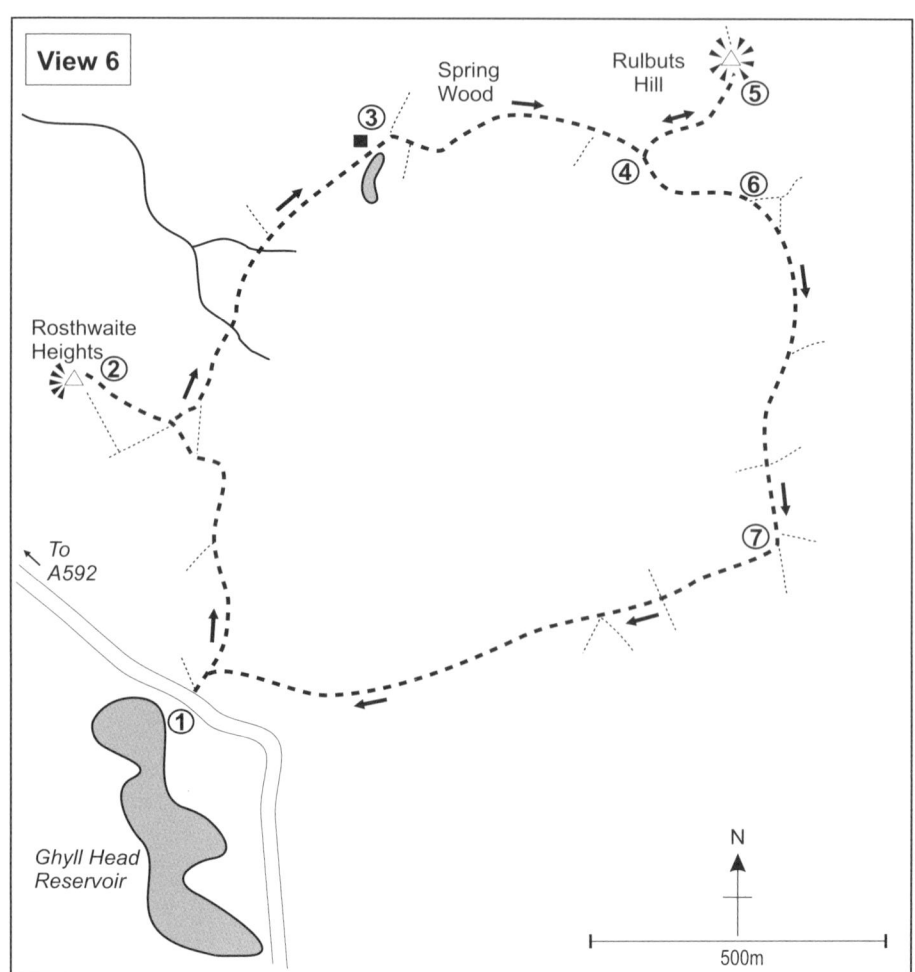

Statue at Rosthwaite Farm

3. Turn right, signed 'Winster', shortly forking left on the main gravel track rising through woodland, full of bluebells and other wild flowers in season. Follow the track through a gate and out of the wood.

4. At the top of the track turn left at a finger post signed 'Rulbuts Hill' and follow the path to the highest point. The path is marked by white topped posts after you reach the open fell.

   Rulbuts Hill is classified as a TUMP, hills of any height with a drop of at least 30 metres or more on all sides. The name TUMP stands for Thirty & Upward Metres Prominence and there are over 16,000 in Britain. The view extends from Morecambe Bay to the south to the head of Windermere (lake) to the north with the mountains of the central Lake District beyond. See plate 8, page 52. The beautiful Winster Valley is spread out to the east, with the Howgills beyond. Is it as good as nearby Orrest Head and Gummer's

How? You will have to decide that for yourself but it is certainly much quieter than those popular viewpoints, so you stand a good chance of being able to enjoy it in peace.

5. After you have had your fill of the view, return to the track and turn left signed 'Winster'. The track leads downhill to a fork.

6. Take the track forking right to reach a T-junction after 50 yards. Turn right and walk along the track for about 600 yards.

7. Watch for an obvious track on the left, starting through a tall gate and signed as a public right of way. Do not take this but continue for 10 yards and then turn right on a grassy path, marked by a yellow arrow on a low post. Leave the wooded area through a gate and after 50 yards go ahead at a cross-path. Stay on the main path, ignoring paths on the left, to eventually reach a T-junction with the path along which this route started. Turn left back to the start.

View 7: Gummer's How
One of the best panoramic views of the Lake District from Coniston Fells to Morecambe Bay

This is a straightforward out and back walk to the prominent and popular crag overlooking the southern end of Windermere (lake). Although short, the final ascent of Gummer's How rises sharply with excellent views on the way up and the reward of a magnificent 360° panorama at the top. Gummer's How is 321 metres (1,053 feet) above sea level but the walk starts at 210 metres so the ascent is only about 100 metres (330 feet). The hill is surrounded by open access land but other routes to the east are inadvisable as the terrain is very boggy.

What you need to know	
Walking distance	2 km. 1½ miles. Height gain: 100 m. 330 feet
Map	OS Explorer OL7 The English Lakes South-eastern area
Starting point	Gummer's How Forestry Commission car park at Fell Foot Brow. Grid reference: SD389876
How to get there	From the A592 6½ miles south of Bowness and one mile north of the junction with the A590 at Newby Bridge, take a road east signed 'Cartmell Fell Bowland Bridge' for about ¾ mile to Gummer's How car park on the right
Refreshments	None on the route. There is a café at Fell Foot Park

Walk Directions

1. Take the clear path on the left near the top of the car park. This shortly returns to the road. Go ahead on the path opposite signed 'Gummer's How ½ mile' for about ¼ mile.

The board on the right tells of how cattle are used to manage the habitat. The view of Lakeside to the left immediately opens up before the path climbs upwards. Take your time as you go up as the view to the south and west unfolds (see plate 9, page 53).

2. Cross a small stream and take the stepped path ascending ahead.

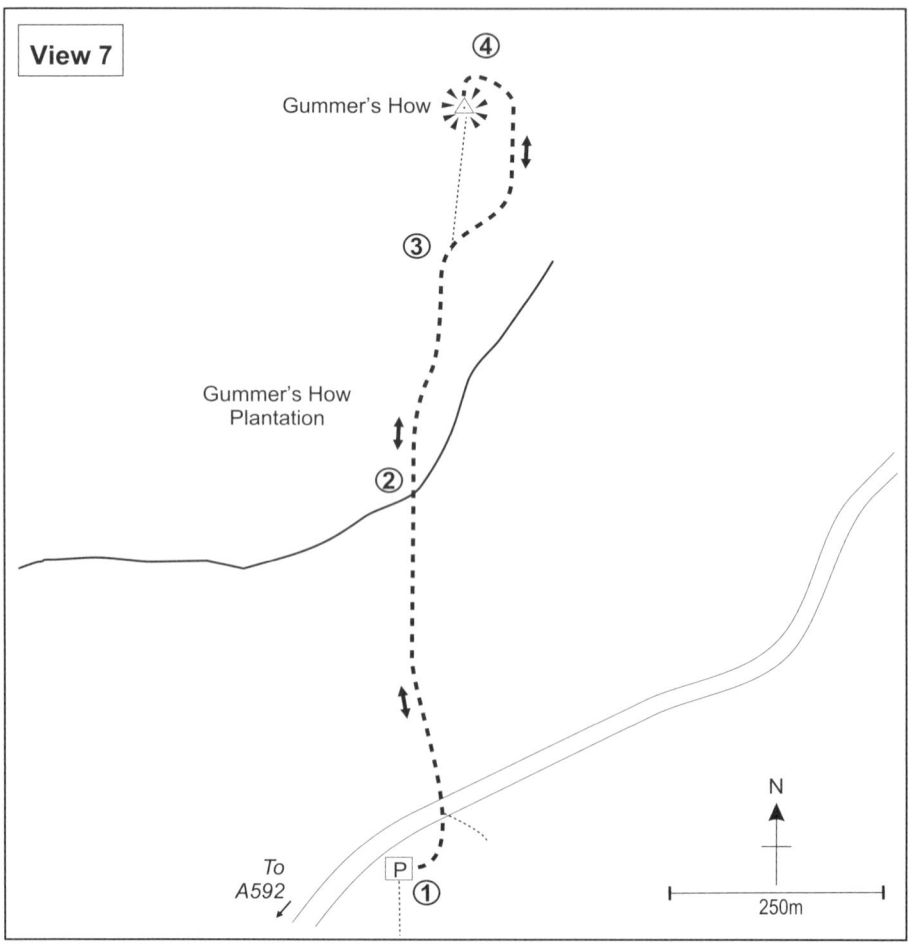

From Lakeside on the opposite shore of the lake, Windermere Lake Cruises operate boats the full length of the lake calling at Bowness and Waterhead. Lakeside station was built in 1869 by the old Furness Railway. You can travel there from Haverthwaite on the Lakeside and Haverthwaite Railway. Also at the station is the Aquarium of the Lakes.

*Lakeside may also be reached by the summer ferry (May-Oct) from nearby Fell Foot Park on the A592 (Grid reference: SD381870). Fell Foot is operated by the National Trust (**www.nationaltrust.org.uk/fell-foot**) and is ideal for a family visit on the shore of the lake. There is a children's adventure playground and you may hire a rowing boat at the Boathouse café.*

The river Leven can be seen leaving the south of the lake to enter Morecambe Bay at Greenodd.

3. At a fence corner on the right take a path along the left hand side of the fence marked with a yellow arrow on a post. Up the crags ahead takes you to the top of Gummer's How via a minor scramble: only for the adventurous. Instead, follow the path shown by yellow arrows to the summit.

Gummer's How is a Marilyn with no neighbouring peaks to block the excellent 360° vista which encompasses the Coniston Fells to the west and Morecambe Bay to the south. Go a little west towards the lake for the view to take in the full length of Windermere (see plate 10, page 53) and the central fells beyond. For more information about Marilyns see View 14.

The triangulation pillar at the summit is 1.2 metres high with a circular brass plate set into the top with grooves for mounting a theodolite. Triangulation is a surveying method that uses a theodolite to measure the angles in a triangle formed by three points. Using trigonometry and the measured length of just one side, the other distances in the triangle are calculated and these are then used as one side of a new triangle and the process is repeated to form a chain of triangles. The hill-top network of trig points was built and measured between 1936 and 1962 and used by the Ordnance Survey to produce new maps of the country. The

Scramble up to Gummer's How

surveying method has now been superseded by satellite-based GPS measurements.

4. Return the same way.

Plate 1: Crummock Water

Plate 2: Buttermere – The Sentinels

Plate 3: The length of Buttermere

Plate 4: Windermere from Claife Viewing Station

Plate 5: The Wasdale Screes

Plate 6: Windermere from Queen Adelaide's Hill

Plate 7: Windermere from Rosthwaite Heights

Plate 8: Windermere from Rulbuts Hill

Plate 9: The Southern Reaches of Windermere from Gummer's How
Plate 10: Windermere from Gummer's How

Plate 11: The View from Helsington Church

Plate 12: Windermere from Jenkin Crag

Plate 13: Holehird Gardens

Plate 14: Orrest Head Viewpoint

Plate 15: Ullswater from Heugh Scar

Plate 16: The Cockpit Stone Circle

Plate 17: Coniston Water from Brantwood

Plate 18: Derwent Water from Castle Crag

Plate 19: Grasmere from Loughrigg Terrace

Plate 20: Loughrigg Tarn and the Langdale Fells

Plate 21: Heron Pike and Rydal Water

Plate 22: The Vale of St. John and Blencathra from Wren Crag

Plate 23: Skiddaw and Bassenthwaite Lake from High Rigg

Plate 24: Tarn Hows and Coniston Water from Black Crag

Plate 25: Lingmoor Fell and the High Fells from Black Crag

Plate 26: Ullswater from Arnison Crag

Plate 27: The Central Lakeland Mountains from Lingmoor Fell
  Plate 28: Blea Tarn, the Langdale Pikes and Side Pike

Plate 29: South from Gowbarrow Fell

Plate 30: Ullswater from Gowbarrow Fell

Plate 31: Derwent Water from Walla Crag

Plate 32: The Jaws of Borrowdale from Friar's Crag

View 8: Sizergh and Helsington
A panorama across the Lakes

This is a relatively easy walk with a small climb up to the church. It starts at Sizergh Castle before visiting Brigsteer wood, ancient woodland important for the variety of wildlife and plants. Then it goes on to isolated Helsington Church, and one of the finest viewpoints in the southern Lake District. In August 2016 the area was included in an extended Lake District National Park.

What you need to know	
Walking distance	4½ km. 3 miles Height gain: 110 m. 360 feet
Map	OS Explorer OL7 The English Lakes South-eastern area
Starting point	Sizergh Castle Car Park (closes at 7pm, no charge at the time of writing but a charge may be imposed in the future for non-members of the National Trust). Grid reference: SD498878
How to get there	From the A591 take the A590 signed 'Lake District Peninsulars' towards Barrow. After about 200 yards take the first road on the right signed 'Sizergh Castle' and follow this to the car park
Alternative starting points	Small car park (at point 2), on the minor road from Levens to Brigsteer, Grid reference: SD489876 and Helsington Church (at point 6), reached by taking the minor road signed 'Brigsteer' on the A591 south of Kendal, Grid reference: SD488889
Refreshments	Excellent Café at the Visitor Centre

Sizergh Castle

Walk Directions

1. At the far end of the car park, to the left of the Visitor Centre, go through a kissing gate onto a track. Turn left signed 'Brigsteer Wood 15 mins' and immediately go through another gate and along the walled and hedged path. Continue through two more gates, the second with large eroded limestone stoops (gate posts). Follow the track ahead onto open pasture with a wall on the left to another two gates, the last one also with limestone stoops.

   The limestone gate stoops were quarried across the valley on the wooded ridge of Whitbarrow. Between these two sets of stoops, to your left, is the old Sizergh Estate deer park boundary.

2. Through the gate, cross the lane. Go ahead through a small car park. Do not take the adjacent path to the left going through a gate with yet more stoops. Follow the track ahead into Brigsteer Wood. After 150 yards pass through a gate and then past a board describing the wood. Continue ahead on the track for 50 yards and the fork right on a path going gently uphill.

If you take a different path through the wood just head downhill to reach a track near the western boundary of the wood and follow it to the end of

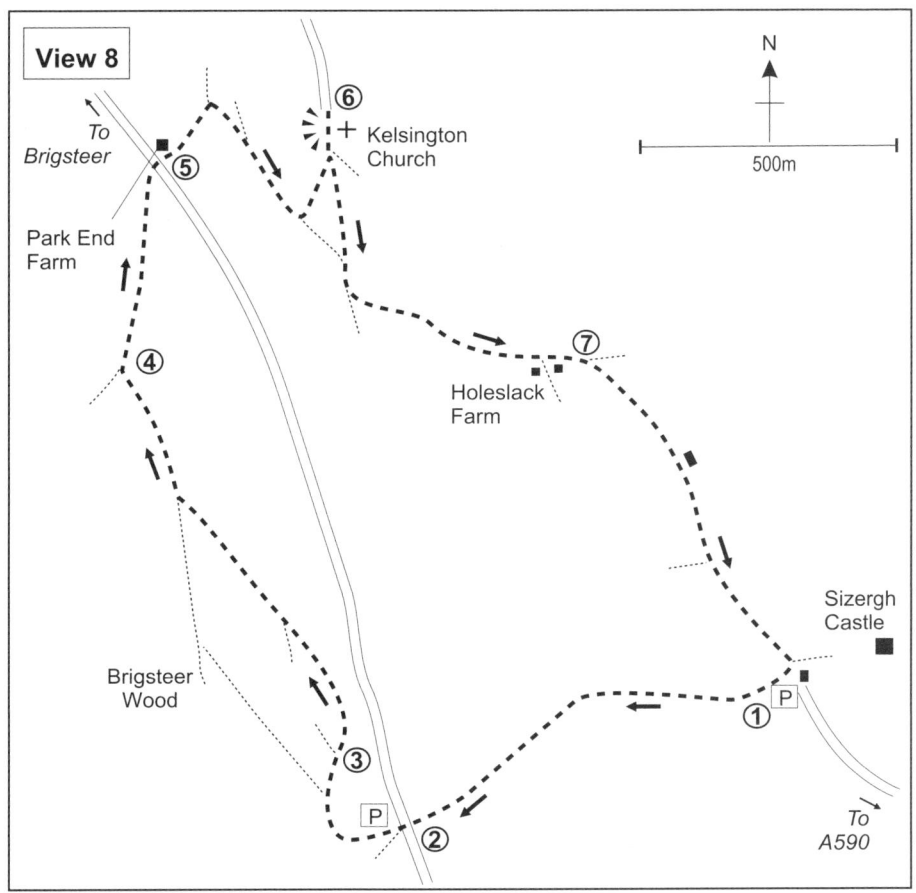

Limestones stoops

the wood at point 4. The ancient woodland is important for the variety of flora and fauna thriving here including the rare fritillary butterfly.

3. After 100 yards fork right again. After a further 400 yards the track descends through the wood. Join a more substantial gravel track to a gate out of the wood.

   To the left is Park End Moss, a recently created wetland nature reserve with cows grazing to prevent coarse grass overwhelming the area. From the bird hide you might see bitterns, marsh harrier, hen harrier, osprey and lapwing.

4. Enter a field and turn right. Ahead is Park End Farm with its traditional Westmorland circular chimney stack. Initially walk along the right hand

side of the field and then bear left away from the wall towards the farm to a gate onto the lane.

In 1974 the historic county of Westmorland was abolished and its former area was combined with Cumberland and parts of Lancashire and Yorkshire to form the county of Cumbria. Westmorland is still used in the name of some organisations and businesses such as the Westmorland Gazette.

5. Cross the lane and take the signed path ahead through three small gates and up to the left-hand corner of a field. Go through a gate and up the walled track to the right. At the end of the wall go ahead a few yards to a cross path. Turn right through woodland. At the end of the wood go ahead across an open area towards a copse on the left. Bear left in front of this to a gravel track in front of a wall. Turn left to the viewpoint at Helsington Church.

The view from the church (plate 11, page 54) is across the Lyth Valley with Morecambe Bay visible to the south and Whitbarrow Scar across the valley. Gummer's How (View 7) is visible beyond. To the right are the Coniston Fells, Scafell Pike and the Langdale Pikes. The toposcope shows the features of the view.

St John's Church was built in 1726 from an endowment by John Jackson of nearby Holeslack Farm and so its isolated position owes much to the proximity of the farm which is passed shortly. The Church serves the nearby village of Brigsteer.

There are some interesting features in the church principally a mural painted at the east end in 1919 just after the first world war by Marion de Saumarez. It shows kneeling angels at prayer and the inscription on the panelling beneath the painting says 'To the glory of God and in memory of all faithful departed especially those who gave their lives in the Great War 1914-1918'. She also undertook another war memorial painting at a church in Suffolk near her home. At the back of the church is the organ made by Samuel Renn of Manchester in the 19th century. It was purchased for the church for £35 in 1902.

Helsington Church

Westmorland Chimneys at Holeslack Farm

6. From the church, return along the track with the wall on your left. At a left-hand bend follow the main track signed 'Sizergh' and go through a gate. Pass Holeslack Farm on your right, with more Westmorland chimneys. Continue on the track passing to the left of farm buildings.

7. At the end of a high wall on your right, turn right on a signed path down steps into a wood. At a barn on the left, bear right through a gate and down a track. At the end of the field go ahead through a gate back to Sizergh Castle.

   The Sizergh Estate was gifted to the National Trust in 1950 by the Strickland family, who still live in part of the castle. Catherine Parr, the sixth and last wife of King Henry VIII and a relative of the Stricklands, is thought to have lived here after her first husband died in 1533. She was already twice-widowed and childless when she married Henry VIII in 1543.

View 9: Jenkin Crag
Views of Winermere

Starting almost at the head of Windermere, this walk begins with a gentle stroll by the lake passing the site of a Roman fort and through a nature reserve with a wonderful display of wild flowers in season. This should get the blood flowing for a short but energetic climb to a spectacular viewpoint on Jenkin Crag before the route returns to Waterhead, passing Stagshaw Gardens.

What you need to know	
Walking distance	4½ km. 3 miles Height gain: 120 m. 400 feet
Map	OS Explorer OL7, The English Lakes South-eastern area
Starting point	Waterhead. Grid reference: NY376032
How to get there	The walk starts at the Ambleside Waterhead car park (charge) close to the steamer pier. From the A591, Windermere Ambleside road, branch left at traffic lights to the car park on the right. Waterhead is well-served by buses including the 555 and 599 services, particularly in the summer when the service is more frequent
Alternative starting point	Low Fold car park (charge) on the A591 about half way between Ambleside and Waterhead, almost opposite a large garden centre. Grid reference: NY377038. You would then start the walk at point 4 and could do a slightly shortened version of the walk returning along the A591 and omitting the visit to Galava fort
Refreshments	There is a wide choice at Waterhead including the Wateredge Inn with gardens leading down to the water

Refreshments cont'd	and spectacular views across the lake. There is a café at the garden centre near point 4. An unusual alternative refreshment stop is the youth hostel at Waterhead, housed in old hotel buildings with another superb view across the lake. Youth hostels have changed a lot since my young days and this one has a café with a bar serving a good choice of local ales: open between noon and 9pm. The food is tasty and reasonably priced and you can eat outside on the terrace to enjoy the view. The youth hostel is passed during point 11

Waterhead

Walk Directions

1. Turn right out of the public car park and pass the Wateredge Inn on your left. After about 50 yards turn left into a park and walk to the lake. Turn right to walk beside the lake. At the far end of the park, when the path

turns right back to the road, go through a metal kissing gate in the wall to Borran's Field containing the remains of the Roman fort. A second kissing gate, near the road, leads you past a National Trust display panel.

Galava fort is now thought to have been built in the late 90s AD in the reign of Emperor Trajan. It was manned by five hundred auxiliaries but it is not really accurate to imagine Romans shivering under Lakeland drizzle trying to suppress rebellious locals. To begin with they did come from other parts of the Western Roman Empire such as Gaul and North Africa. Later the auxiliaries were recruited locally, signing on for 25 years. The fort mostly existed peacefully with the civilian population and the main problem was marauding Picts and Scots. The fort was abandoned around 400 AD as the Roman Empire collapsed. The name of the site, Borran's Field, is from the Norse meaning heap of stones, which suggests the state it was in when

Galava Roman Fort

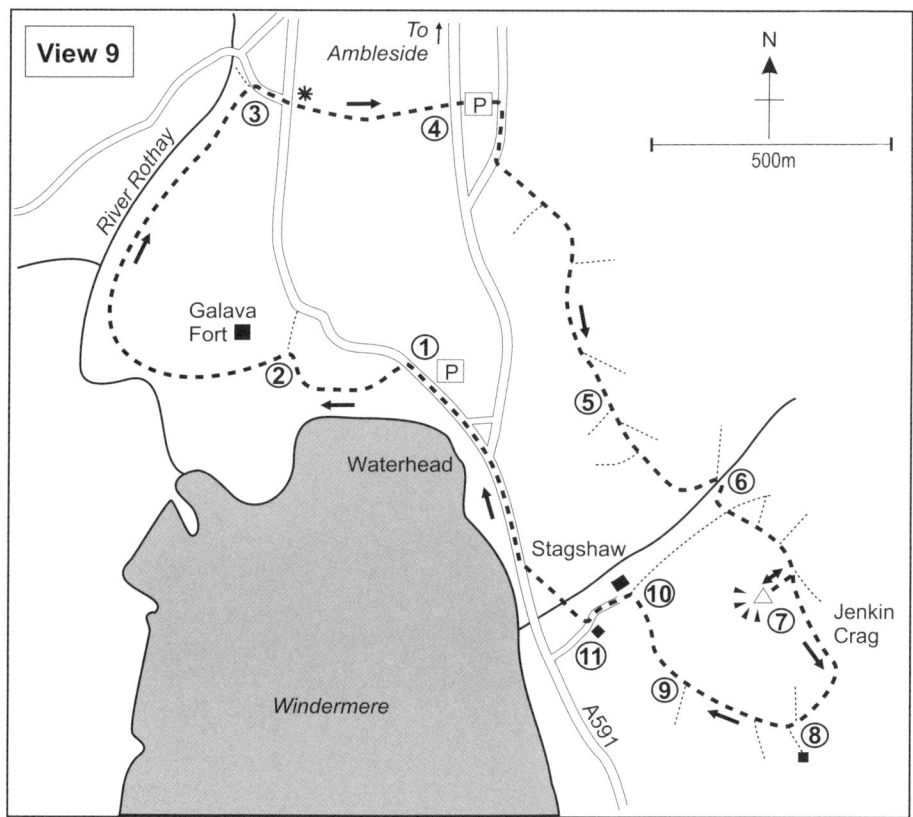

Norse settlers moved in after the Romans departed. It was bought by the National Trust in 1912 to protect it from house building and excavated by R.G. Collingworth between 1914 and 1920. There has been no substantial excavation inside the fort since Collingworth's day and presumably other remains, such as the bath-house, may be found one day.

2. Bear half left across the field, inspecting the remains with their information plaques as you go, to gates into Birdhouse Meadow. Follow the path as it bends right beside the river, past the confluence of the river Brathay and river Rothay, to reach a gate. Through the gate, turn right to a road.

(Note: the path across Birdhouse Meadow may be flooded in winter. Also, the path by the river is not a public footpath and access is at the discretion of the landowner. It is a popular path but could be withdrawn. If the path is impassable for either reason, go back and through a gate from Borrans Field on to the road and turn left to pick up the route again at * below.)

3. Turn right along the road to reach a road junction. Cross the road ahead (*) and maintain direction along a fenced path that emerges on a main road opposite Low Fold car park.

4. Cross the road and car park to a lane at the rear and turn right. Take the first left, signed 'Jenkins Crag-Skelghyll and Troutbeck'. Follow the surfaced track up and when it forks take the right branch, signed 'Jenkyn's Crag'. The track contours along the hillside with superb views on the right over the head of Windermere and up the Langdale Valley. At the next fork again take the right option, signed 'Skelghyll Woods', to continue along the hillside.

5. On entering Skelghyll Woods ignore a path on the right to continue uphill on the main path. Pass the private entrance to Skelghyll Woods and then fork left on a bridleway. Continue uphill with a beck on your right.

6. Follow the main path round to the right to cross the beck at a bridge. Ignore all paths on the right and left and continue up to Jenkin Crag. Turn right through a gap in the wall at the Jenkins Crag sign to the viewpoint.

Jenkin Crag has magnificent views over the head of Windermere and the fells beyond. See plate 12, page 54. Slightly to the left, on the far side of the lake is Blelham Tarn. Looking to the right are the Coniston Fells and further to the right beyond Black Crag (View 16) is Wetherlam and, on a clear day, you can see Crinkle Crags, Bowfell and, from the rocks to your left, the Langdale Pikes. The exact spelling of the name Jenkin Crag seems to vary. On the Ordnance Survey map it is called Jenkin Crag. The sign on the track near the start directs us to Jenkin's Crag and further up the spelling has changed to Jenkyn's Crag - with and without apostrophes.

7. From the viewpoint return towards the main path. Do **not** go through the gap in the wall onto the main path. Instead, just before the wall, take a smaller path on the right downhill. This soon curves right and goes steeply downhill through a wooded area.

8. Turn right on a crossing path leading from a house.

9. When the main path turns very sharply left, maintain direction on a smaller path. Follow this to join a track.

10. Turn left passing Stagshaw Gardens on the right.

    Stagshaw Gardens, passed towards the end of this walk, was created by the late C. H. D. Acland, a keen gardener, who was regional agent for the National Trust for nearly thirty years. An area of scrubby woodland was transformed into a series of glades with rhododendrons, azaleas and a wide variety of other shrubs thriving under the thinned oaks. It is essentially a spring garden and is open every day from April until the end of June from 10.00am to 6.30pm, daily. In the summer, from July to October, it is open by appointment only. (Send s.a.e. to Property Office, St Catherine's, Patterdale Road, Windermere LA23 1NH.) Telephone: 015394 46027.

11. Just after a stone barn on the left turn right on a path between a wall and a fence and follow this to a road. Turn right. There is a footway on the opposite side of this busy road. At the traffic lights bear left back to the car park.

View 10: Orrest Head and Holehird
The view that inspired Alfred Wainwright

At 238 metres (784 feet) above sea level, Orrest Head is deservedly very popular. It is accessible from Windermere village and is one of the first fells to be encountered when approaching the Lake District on the A591. Alfred Wainwright said the sight of Windermere (lake) and the high fells are a truly magnificent view and who am I to argue with him. The view from Holehird Gardens is very nearly as superb, enhanced by the beautiful garden setting. Admission to the gardens is free but donations are welcome. Only assistance dogs are allowed at Holehird, so with a dog you should visit just Orrest Head. There are many routes up Orrest Head and the best alternatives are given in the directions for this walk.

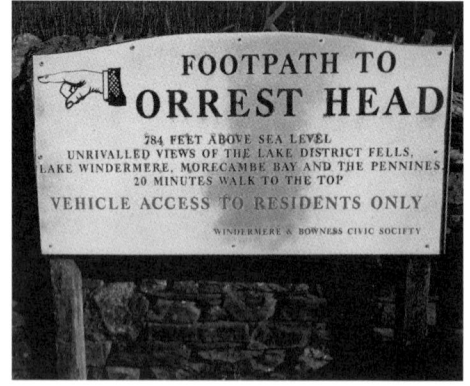

Invitation to Orrest Head

What you need to know	
Walking distance	6½ km. 4 miles. Height gain: 130 m. 450 feet; for shorter versions visiting just Orrest Head see points 2 and 4
Map	OS Explorer OL7 The English Lakes South-eastern area
Starting point	Windermere railway station. Grid reference: SD413986
How to get there	Take the A591 from Kendal to Windermere. There is a small amount of on street parking on the A591 (some

How to get there cont'd	time limited). Alternatively, use the car park at the station or Broad Street car park at the lower (southern) end of Windermere village (both charge). Even better take the train or bus. The bus station is adjacent to the railway station and is served by many routes including the 555 service from Lancaster to Keswick
Alternative starting point	Holehird gardens, signed from the A592 ¾ mile north of the junction with the A591. You will then start the walk at point 6 taking the path on the right beyond the reception to a gate at the top of the garden
Refreshments	A very wide choice in Windermere. Only drinks (tea, coffee, hot chocolate) are available at Holehird gardens

Walk Directions

1. From Windermere railway and bus station cross the A591. By the traffic light controlled pedestrian crossing, take the well signed 'Footpath to Orrest Head' to the left of the Windermere Hotel. The 20 minute estimate of time to reach Orrest Head may be seen as a target if you take the short route described at point 2. After 40 yards, fork left signed 'A592 Troutbeck Rd'.

Much confusion has been caused to visitors arriving in Windermere village expecting to find the identically named lake. This is also the case for other meres and waters in the Lake District. The village (or a small town which likes to be known as a village) of Windermere is very much the product of the railway era. The railway stopped at the hamlet of Birthwaite but I suppose that didn't sound very attractive to early tourists so it was renamed Windermere to emphasize its connection with the lake even though this is more than a mile away. It was originally planned that the railway should continue on to Ambleside and Grasmere and then over Dunmail Raise to Keswick. The extension was prevented by the vehement protests of Wordsworth, among others. If the plans had been carried through then Windermere almost certainly would not have developed as much as it has.

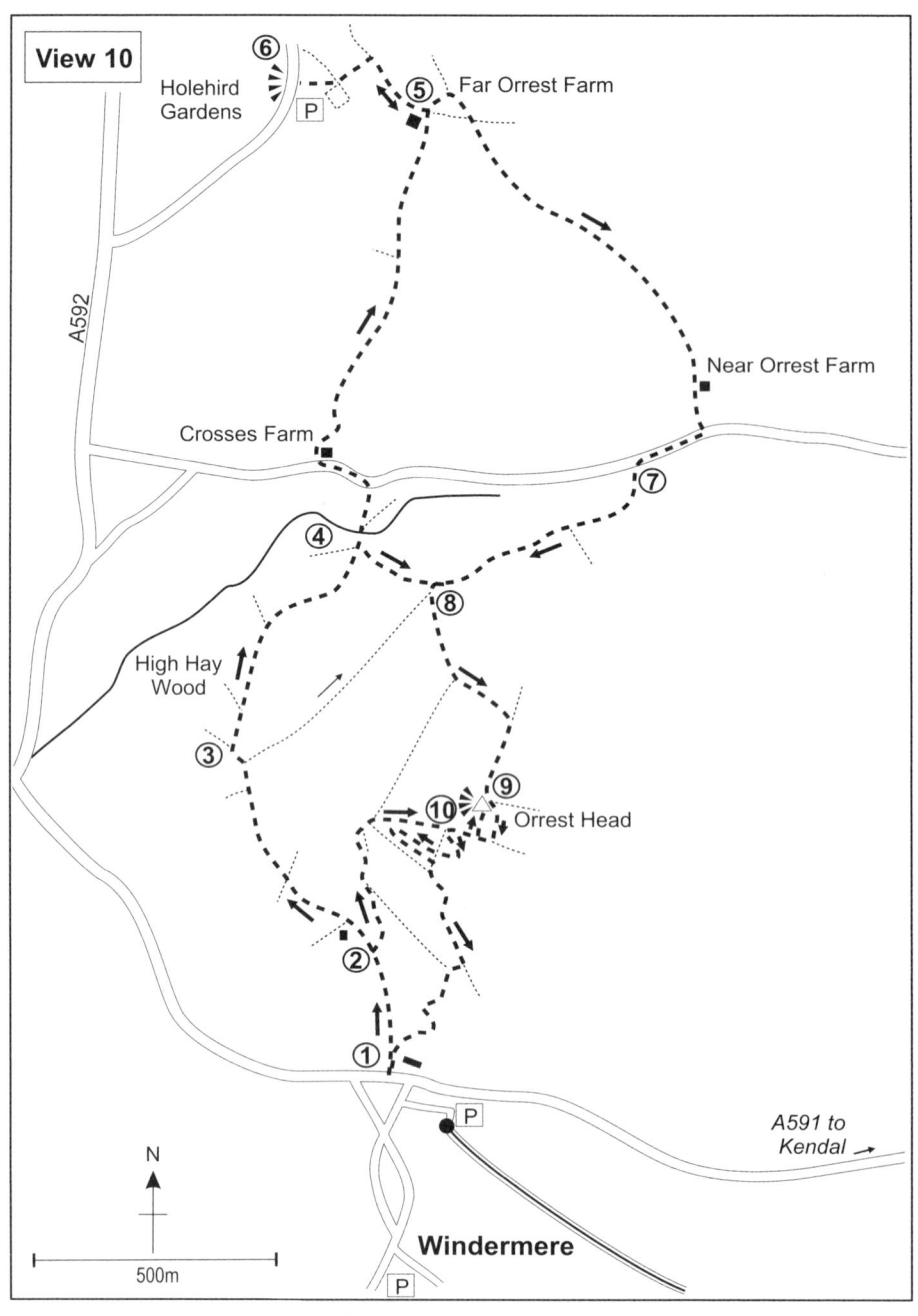

2. After about 300 yards, at a finger post, continue ahead signed 'Kirkstone Road ½ mile'. (If you want to take a short route to Orrest head, omitting Holehird, turn right signed 'Orrest Head ½ mile' and follow the way-marked path up Orrest Head, and return following the directions given at point 9. This makes the walk only 1¼ miles long.) To continue on the longer route, pass to the rear of Windermere Preparatory School and continue ahead on a path with a metal fence on the left. Cross a tarmac driveway and take the signed path ahead to the left of the entrance to Elleray bank. Ignore a path on the right signed 'Causeway Farm ½ mile' and continue ahead signed 'Patterdale road 500 yards St. Katherines' for 35 yards.

3. Turn right through a metal gate on a permitted footpath into High Hay Wood. Go through a wooden kissing gate and walk with a wall initially on your left and then on your right. Fork right up a field (not left to two bridges) still with the wall on your right and through another wooden kissing gate. Turn left, now with a wall on your left.

4. At a finger post you again have a choice. The main route to Holehird continues ahead through a wooden kissing gate signed 'Crosses Farm 170 yards'. (If you want to take another route also omitting Holehird, turn right signed 'Orrest Head ½ mile' and follow the path up the left hand side of a field to a finger post at point 8, making the walk 2 miles long.) To continue to Holehird, go through the kissing gate, cross a footbridge and immediately fork left. Turn left at a lane for 200 yards. Immediately after Crosses Farm turn right on a track signed 'Troutbeck 1½ mile'. Go through a metal farm gate, across a field and into a second field. When the farm track turns left, continue ahead between rock outcrops to a wall corner. Take the track ahead to a gate just before Far Orrest Farm. Now leave the track to go ahead and pass to the right of a barn.

5. Turn left, signed 'A592 via Dodds Lane ½ mile', on a tarmac farm drive. Cross a cattle grid and after 40 yards at a very small cairn turn left down a field to a stile and gate at the bottom left hand corner. Through the gate you enter Holehird Gardens. Bear left and then right to take a path down to a tarmac drive. Turn left to the viewpoint on the right and the reception and walled garden on the left.

The bank on the right is covered in a splendid display of daffodils in the spring. The Lakeland Horticultural Society's 17 acre hillside gardens at Holehird include a great variety of trees and shrubs, extensive rock and heather gardens, a walled garden and four national collections. The gardens are open all year round and the reception is manned from Easter to October. Admission is by donation. The view from the garden from a well placed seat encompasses the lake and the fells (see plate 13, page 55). There is a plaque to help you identify the peaks.

6. From Holehird, return up the garden and through the fell gate, over the stile and up to the small cairn on the farm drive. Turn right, over the cattle grid, to return to Far Orrest Farm. Now take the path sharp left signed 'Near Orrest Farm ½ mile' and immediately bear right up a small slope to a gate. Go through the gate and a second smaller gate. Turn right signed 'Near Orrest Farm' along the right hand side of a field. Follow the wall on the right. As it bends left go through a gate on the right, cross a track and through another gate. Ignore an immediate gate on the right and follow the wall on the right as it first bends right and then left to a gate on the right. Through this gate bear left in the direction shown on a post across a large field to cross a stile by the fifth large tree counting from the left. This tree is on the far side of the wall at a wall junction. Continue along the left hand side of the next field, over a stile and ahead to a stile six yards to the right of a gate. Through another gate bear right of the buildings of Near Orrest Farm, through a small gate and go along the left hand side of a field to a lane. Turn right for 200 yards.

7. Take the track on the left signed 'Public Footpath', over a stile by a metal gate. Cross a stream and follow a wall on the right uphill to a gate on the right. Through the gate bear left uphill following yellow arrows on posts to a finger post.

8. Of the two paths on the left (on the right if you have just come up from point 4) take the left-hand one signed 'Orrest Head ¼ mile'. Over a ladder stile, bear left uphill to a gate. Through the gate, turn right signed 'Orrest Head 150 yards'.

There are superb views in all directions from the summit. In 1930 Alfred Wainwright climbed up Orrest Head after alighting from the train at Windermere station for his first view of the Lakeland mountains. The view over the lake to the fells to the north and west inspired him to write his series of 'Pictorial Guides to the Lakeland Fells'. (See plate 14, page 55 for the view from near the toposcope or plaque). He preferred the term Lakeland to the currently more widely used Lake District. The plaque identifying the peaks is inscribed with a quote from Wainwright extolling the magnificent view. Make sure you look to the east for the Howgills and the Pennines and, on a clear day, to the south for Morecambe Bay.

9. From the viewpoint you may take the popular rocky path heading down towards Windermere village. However, an easier route is to go left for 20 yards and take a path downhill marked by a white arrow on a post. At a wall turn right and go through a metal kissing gate to continue ahead.

    Just through the kissing gate note the stone on the right commemorating Arthur Henry Heywood whose family gave Orrest Head to the public.

10. At a wall, turn left down a track with the wall initially on your right. This is gently graded for wheelchair use. It goes round bends and 20 yards after entering the wood you may take a rough shortcut down to the left or continue down the gently graded track to join another track and then go left, signed 'Windermere Village'. This soon becomes surfaced and wends its way downhill to the start.

View 11: Heugh Scar and Heughscar Hill
A ridge walk with views over Ullswater from the north

Starting near Pooley Bridge at the northern end of Ullswater the walk climbs gently up to Heugh Scar and then along the limestone ridge to Heughscar Hill, with views over Ullswater all the way. After that there is an enigmatic stone circle, one of many such structures in the Lake District. It was already ancient when it was passed by Roman soldiers along High Street. It is amazing to think that it was already about 3,000 years old when they came this way. I wonder what they made of it?

What you need to know	
Walking distance	4½ km. 3 miles Height gain: 150 m. 500 feet
Map	OS Explorer OL5 The English Lakes North-eastern area
Starting point	Roadside parking at Roehead. Grid reference: NY478236
How to get there	From the B5320 Pooley Bridge Eamont Bridge road at the eastern end of Pooley Bridge, beside St. Paul's Church, take a road to the south signed 'Howtown 4 Martindale 5'. At a crossroads go ahead on Roe Head Lane signed 'Hill Croft ¼' and park on the left just before the end of the road
Refreshments	Pubs and café in Pooley Bridge. The tea room by the bridge is particularly well-placed with a garden overlooking the River Eamont

Walk Directions

1. Go ahead, through a gate, onto a track signed 'Helton'. After 70 yards, turn left on a smaller track with grass along the middle between deep ruts. After 30 yards, branch left on a small grassy path towards trees. At the trees, bear right to walk uphill with trees and a wall on your left. Look back

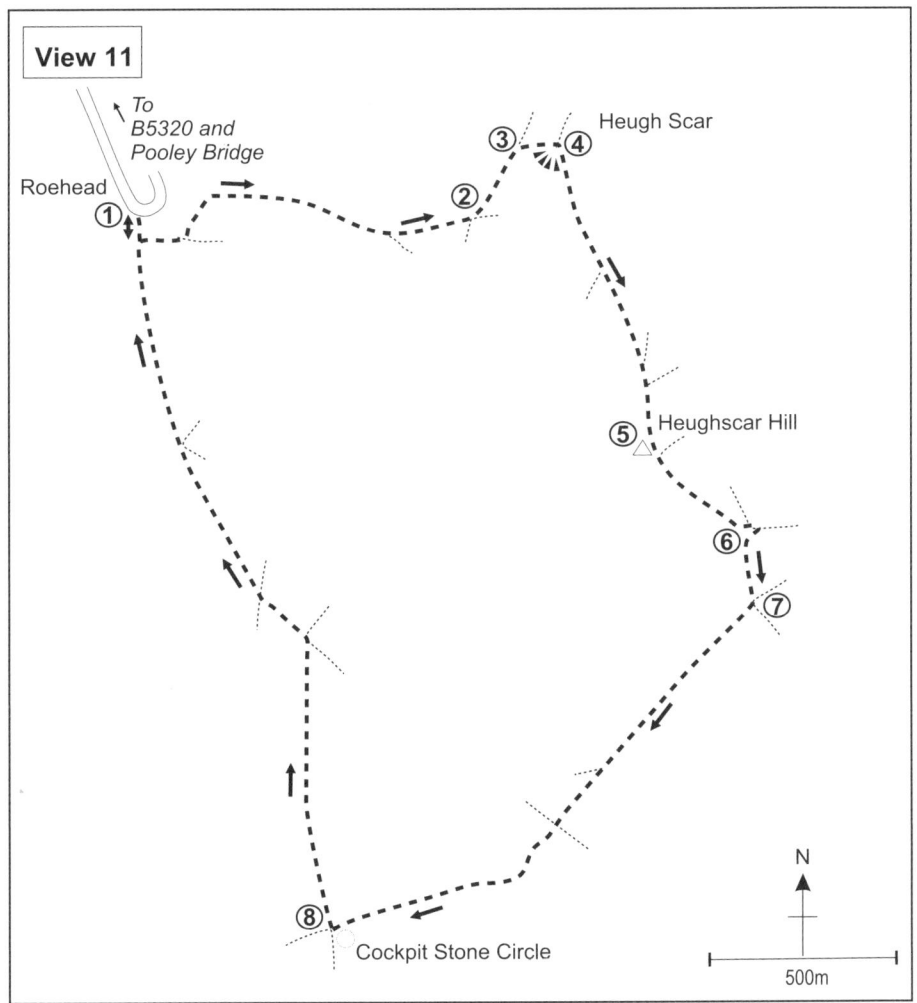

for views over Ullswater and the fells. At the end of the wall continue ahead up a grassy path. At a fork bear left on the main path towards the prominent rocky outcrop of Heugh Scar.

2. At a major cross-path turn left towards Heugh Scar.

3. Just after passing below Heugh Scar, branch right on a small path ascending to Heugh Scar.

   Heugh Scar is a limestone outcrop, fairly rare in the Lake District and more usually found in the Yorkshire Dales. There are extensive views over the northern end of Ullswater to the Helvellyn range with Striding Edge visible on a clear day. See plate 15, page 56. In front is Gowbarrow Fell (View 19) and Place Fell to the left of the lake. Across the lake to the right of Gowbarrow are Great and Little Mell with Blencathra beyond.

4. Continue ahead, initially along the top of Heugh Scar onto the rather flat summit of Heughscar Hill, where there is an outcrop of small limestones.

5. Follow the path curving left to the corner of a plantation of trees.

6. At the trees turn right downhill.

   Views to the Pennines in the east now open up. To the south-east are the Howgills in the Yorkshire Dales National Park. This is separated from the Lake District National Park only by a narrow band encompassing the M6 motorway.

7. After about 200 yards, at a cross-path, turn right gently downhill. After about 400 yards, at another cross-path go ahead to reach a stone circle marked as the Cockpit on the Ordnance Survey map.

   The Cockpit Stone Circle is probably the most impressive of a number of prehistoric monuments from the Bronze Age scattered over Moor Divock. It is about 30 yards across and its original purpose is a mystery, but probably had some ritual significance. See plate 16, page 56.

8. Immediately after the Cockpit on your left, turn sharp right on a path heading towards Heugh Scar.

   As you walk down the path another view of Ullswater opens up to the left.

   At a cross-path by a cairn, turn left back to the start of this walk.

The path back to Roehead

View 12: Brantwood and Coniston
The café with the best views

This lovely walk explores the head of Coniston Water climbing gently through the Monk Coniston estate and then above the lake to Brantwood with superb views of Coniston Old Man and the surrounding fells. Brantwood is often described as the most beautifully situated house in England. There is an excellent café with a terrace overlooking the lake and a superb view over Coniston Water. The return is by a cruise across the lake on one of the historic launches. The route is varied and interesting with fantastic views throughout. Early visitors to the Lakes regarded the site of Brantwood as one of the most picturesque in the Lake District.

What you need to know	
Walking distance	6½ km. 4 miles. Height gain: 150 m. 500 feet
Map	OS Explorer OL7 The English Lakes South-eastern area
Starting point	Coniston Sports and Social Club car park, Shepherds Bridge Lane (charge). Grid reference: SD305977
How to get there	On entering Coniston on the A593 from Ambleside, take Shepherds Bridge Lane on the left signed 'Hawkshead The Lake Tarn Hows'. The Coniston Sports and Social Club car park is on the left, 60 yards after Coniston Primary School, or you may be fortunate enough to find a roadside parking spot opposite the school. The 505 bus from Windermere and Ambleside goes to Coniston
Alternative starting points	From the main public car park in Coniston (charge) Grid reference: SD303975, turn right in the direction of Hawkshead and then left along Shepherds Bridge Lane,

Alternative starting points cont'd	OR Monk Coniston car park (charge) Grid reference: SD306978; you would then start at point 6, OR Coniston Pier car park (charge); Grid reference: SD307971 you would the start at point 9
Refreshments	Brantwood Café

Walk Directions

1. Go out of the car park and turn right for 60 yards. Opposite Coniston Primary School turn right on a signed public footpath crossing Yewdale Beck. Over the bridge turn left. Go through a kissing gate and follow the path uphill, passing an unusual crenulated building, once the kennels for the fox hounds of the Monk Coniston estate and now an information point. Continue uphill to the next gate and for about 60 yards after that.

The Dog House

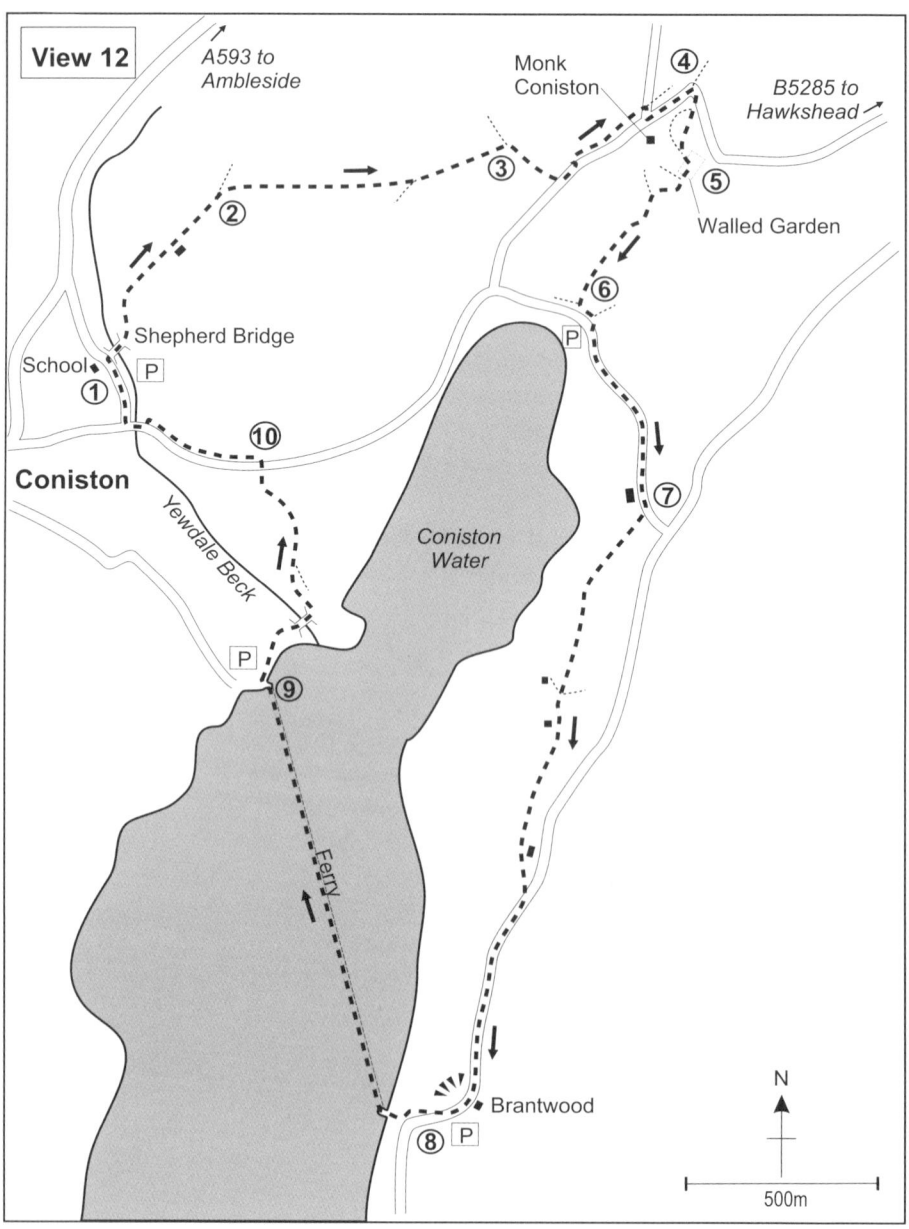

Created by Nature and originally owned by the Monks of Furness Abbey, the estate was skillfully augmented by its Victorian owners; the wealthy families who owned it in the 18th and 19th centuries. The Knott family made their fortune from iron-smelting in the Lake District and Scotland. They owned Monk Coniston from 1769-1835 and planted lots of trees and developed the beautiful parkland. In 1835 the estate was sold to James Garth Marshall. He bought more land to extend the estate and was responsible for creating the iconic but artificial Tarn Hows as well as planting more trees around the hall and across the estate. The estate came on the market in 1930 and Beatrix Potter bought much of the land. She immediately sold half to the National Trust at cost price and left them the rest in her will. They were able to buy the house and garden later to reunite the estate. Monk Coniston house is not open to the public but the route leads through the walled garden.

2. When the wall on the right turns right, turn right to initially follow the wall then up to a gate into a wood. Carry on along the path over the brow of the hill and down the other side with a view of Coniston Water to the right. Continue to a gate onto a track.

3. Turn right, signed 'Tarn Hows Coniston via Waterhead' to a road. Turn left and after 20 yards escape the road on to a permitted bridleway on the left of the road. At a lane turn right, signed 'Monk Coniston 100 yds', back to the road and turn left uphill to continue in the same direction as far as a right hairpin bend.

4. On the apex of the bend turn right through a small wooden gate into the grounds of Monk Coniston Hall and follow the track to the left into the walled garden.

The grounds have an impressive collection of exotic conifers planted largely from the early 19th century. Global explorers gathered many new seeds and plants which wealthy land owners displayed on their estates. There is a seat at the far top corner of the walled garden, an excellent place to rest with a view over the lake also seen as you walk down to the lake.

5. Halfway across the garden turn right and leave the garden through a wooden gate and then bear left on the path signed 'Lake'. Just after 'Jim's Bench' on the right, go through a metal gate out of woodland on the left and continue down towards the lake to a lane.

6. At the lane, with Monk Coniston car park ahead, turn left on a path parallel to the lane. After 30 yards continue on the lane.

7. Just after passing Tent Lodge on the right, turn right signed 'Thurston ¾ mile' through some gates and walk past a converted barn. Go through more gates and continue on the path along the right hand side of three fields. Cross a track leading to buildings on the right and keep ahead through gates to skirt to the left of the next building. Cross a surfaced drive and press on along the path, signed 'Brantwood'. After passing to the right of an enviable house cross a small stream and bear half left. At the end of the hedge on the left continue ahead to rejoin the lane and turn right to Brantwood.

Brant is an old Norse word meaning 'steep' and Brantwood house and grounds are on a steep wooded area overlooking Coniston Water. The house was built at the end of the 18th century – something that planning regulations would never allow today. Brantwood was the home of John Ruskin, poet, artist and social reformer. The house and gardens are open to the public and from the seats on the café's terrace you may take in the excellent view over the lake (see plate 17, page 57). The café is open throughout the year. Telephone: 015394 41396, **www.brantwood.org.uk**

8. Opposite the entrance to Brantwood car park turn right through the Lower Garden to the jetty to catch the launch to Coniston pier.

In 2005 the launches 'Ruskin' and 'Ransome' were converted to solar-electric power and on sunny days the solar panels can provide two-thirds of the power needed to run the boats. There is a Coniston launch timetable in the tea room or at **www.conistonlaunch.co.uk**. *Note that although the the launch runs on all weekends it does not run on all weekdays from early November to early February.*

Steam Yacht Gondola

> *From the end of March to the end of October, if you time it right, you can ride in luxury on the Victorian Steam Yacht Gondola to Coniston via Monk Coniston jetty at the northern end of the lake. Timetables are at* **www.nationaltrust.org.uk/steam-yacht-gondola**

9. With your back to the lake, take a path to the right starting by the boat and bike hire kiosk signed 'Waterhead and Alternative Route to Coniston Village'. At the end of the bay follow the main path bearing left away from the lake. Cross a footbridge and turn left to join a surfaced drive and follow this to a road.

10. Cross the road and turn left along a roadside path. When this path ends, continue along the road for 50 yards. Immediately after a bridge over Yewdale Beck, take the first road on the right, Shepherds Bridge Lane signed 'Skelwith Ambleside', back to the start.

View 13: Castle Crag
Views from the Jaws of Borrowdale

This is a magnificent walk in Borrowdale, a valley that many, including Wainwright, consider to be the very best in this area of outstanding scenery: a lush valley surrounded by towering fells, woods ablaze with colour in autumn, a crystal clear river with its deep and mysterious pools and charming hamlets scattered around. No wonder it is so popular. Without great care and skilful management it could easily be loved to death, so it is fortunate that it is mostly in the care of the National Trust. Castle Crag is one of the prominent jagged teeth in the Jaws of Borrowdale, south of Derwent Water. This short walk is rather energetic as there is a steep ascent and descent, made more difficult near the top of Castle Crag by loose slate. However it is worth it for the superb views over both Derwent Water and Borrowdale.

What you need to know	
Walking distance	5½ km. 3½ miles Height gain: 210 m. 700 feet
Map	OS Explorer OL4 The English Lakes North-western area
Starting point	Grange Café, Grange-in-Borrowdale Grid reference: NY252174
How to get there	Take the B5289 Borrowdale Road, south from Keswick for 4 miles. Turn right over the bridge and through the village. There is some roadside parking at the far side of the village or turn left along a lane to the right of Grange Café signed 'Hollows Farm' to a parking area on the right after 100 yards. From Keswick bus route 78 stops on the B5289 at Grange Bridge and the seasonal 77A goes to Grange
Refreshments	Grange Café, a welcome sight on the return from Castle Crag

Walk Directions

1. Take the lane signed 'Hollows Farm' and 'Seatoller 3m Rosthwaite 2m' to the right of Grange Café.

   As you approach Hollows Farm, Castle Crag is visible to the left between trees.

2. Turn left on a track towards the campsite signed 'Castle Crag ¾ m'. Past the campsite, the track forks. Take the left branch, past a metal barrier towards the river Derwent.

3. Cross the first stream using the footbridge. Ignore a path on the right and after 100 yards go over another footbridge.

River Derwent

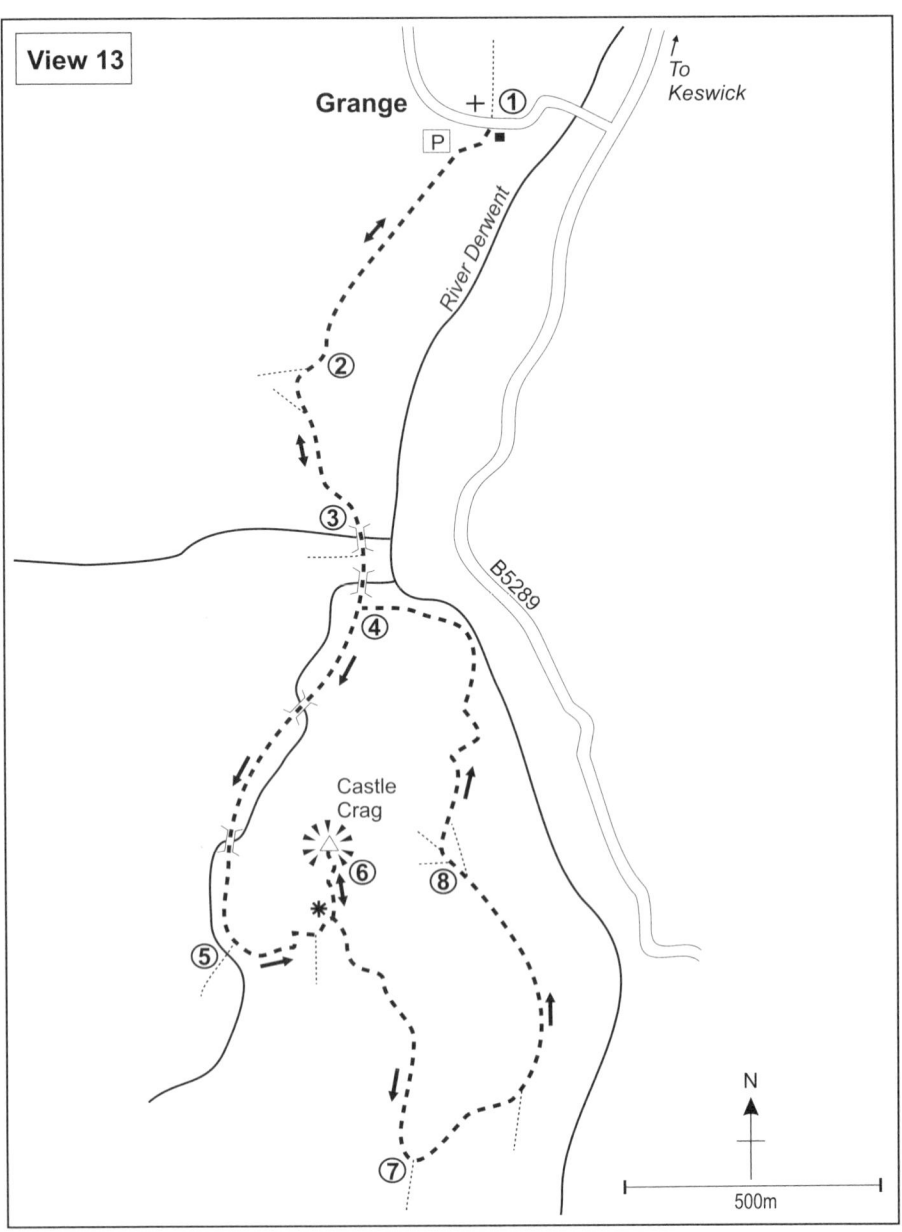

4. Turn right uphill signed 'Seatoller 2 miles Honister 3 miles' with Broadslack Gill on your right. Cross this at another footbridge and continue uphill and through a gate out of the wood. At the end of a wall on the left continue for about 100 yards to cross the gill again.

5. After a further 200 yards, where the path yet again crosses the gill, take a path on your left now with the gill on your right. This curves left uphill, over a stile in a wall and past an inviting seat on the right. It then goes up a stepped path and right through a wooden gate. Turn left at a wall where there is a stile ahead and note a second stile on the right (*), to which you will be returning. The path now zig-zags up through slate debris from the disused quarry on the left and up to the top of Castle Crag.

Castle Crag has magnificient views in all directions, particularly over Derwent Water to Skiddaw beyond and with Kings How and Walla Crag (View 20) to the right (see plate 18, page 57). Looking behind, the view is over the river Derwent and up Borrowdale. It is not surprising that Castle Crag was once crowned by a fort or castle belonging to the Celtic confederation, the Brigantes, which must have been impregnable. It was given to the National Trust in 1920 in memory of the men of Borrowdale who died in the First World War.

6. Return from the top down the zig-zag path and you will see a ladder stile over the wall on your left at (*) noted earlier. Over the stile follow the path down a grassy slope, then a stepped path and through a gate in a wall. Continue downhill into Borrowdale towards the river Derwent and to a track.

Borrowdale stretches from the head of Derwent Water to Seathwaite, which, as every school child knows, is the wettest place in England with 330cm (130 inches) annually, though some of the surrounding fells probably have more. Kept well-watered by this abundant rainfall and fertilised by alluvium from the flooding of the river, the flat land in the bottom of the valley is some of the lushest pasture in the Lake District. Dales such as Borrowdale were very isolated in the past and had a reputation for being unsophisticated, to put it mildly. There are many stories told to illustrate this, such as the one about the cuckoo wall. The inhabitants of the dale noticed that spring always came

Borrowdale

with the cuckoos and so they reasoned that if only the cuckoo could be persuaded to stay in the dale they would enjoy perpetual spring. To this end they built a wall across the valley at Grange to keep the bird in and when the plan failed they decided that they just hadn't built the wall high enough! The local people obviously resented this slur on their intelligence and it is said that if the word 'cuckoo' was said as a Borrowdale man came into a pub, it was enough to start a fight.

7. Turn left and follow the main path. Pass a pile of quarry debris on your left, and after 50 yards ignore a minor path ascending to the right.

8. After a further 10 yards fork right on the main path and after a further 30 yards turn sharp right on a public footpath signed 'Grange'. Follow the path over footbridges and past the campsite back to Grange.

View 14: Loughrigg Fell
Outstanding views every step of the way round a Marilyn

If someone had only one day to walk in the Lakes and wanted to see the best of it, this is the walk I would recommend. Loughrigg Fell is almost isolated from other hills, and from its flanks wonderful views stretch in every direction. There is hardly a step of the walk without a magnificent view to admire. It circumnavigates Loughrigg Fell anti-clockwise, starting along Loughrigg Terrace with a fabulous view over the lake to Helm Crag beyond. The route then descends to walk beside Loughrigg Tarn, often considered the most beautiful tarn in the Lakes. This is followed by a path up to Ivy Crag with breathtaking views of the Langdales and Windermere and then over the shoulder of the fell to descend the northern flank towards the jewel of Rydal Water.

What you need to know	
Walking distance	8 km. 5 miles Height gain: 230 m. 750 feet
Map	OS Explorer OL7, The English Lakes South-eastern area
Starting point	White Moss Walks car park. Grid reference: NY349065
How to get there	How to get there: White Moss Walks car park (charge) is on A591, Ambleside Grasmere road about 2 miles north of Ambleside. Use the southern section, on the left coming from Ambleside. Buses 555 Lancaster to Keswick and the 599 Bowness to Grasmere summer service stop at White Moss
Alternative starting point	Alternative starting point: Near Tarn Foot Lodge (point 7). Grid reference: NY345040 reached from the A593 about 2 miles west of Ambleside, at a sharp left hand bend, bear right along a minor road signed 'High Close' for about half a mile and take the first left just over a bridge to a parking area immediately on the left

| Refreshments | None on the route but numerous and varied pubs and cafés in Grasmere |

Walk Directions

1. Leave the rear of the car park to pass a low wooden barrier and find a roughly surfaced path. Ignore paths on the right to reach the river Rothay on the left and go past a popular picnic area to a footbridge over the river.

   The river flows from Grasmere to Rydal Water.

2. Over the bridge, bear slightly right into White Moss Woods away from the river signed 'Rydal Caves ¾ mile Ambleside 2¾ miles'. Follow the path uphill through the woods and through a gate in a wall.

3. Turn right, signed 'Grasmere 2 miles' up onto Loughrigg Terrace. There are plenty of seats to admire the view over Grasmere as you climb gently.

River Rothay

See plate 19, page 58. Ignore the path on the left at the end of the terrace which leads up steps towards the summit of Loughrigg Fell.

Loughrigg Terrace is very famous with its acclaimed views over Grasmere. The fell beyond the lake is Helm Crag. The rocks on top are supposed, from certain directions, to resemble a lion and a lamb.

Loughrigg is the fell to the north of Ambleside. This undistinguished mass sits at the junction of five major valley systems. It is a Marilyn with no neighbouring peaks to block the views so there are unrivalled panoramas in every direction. There must be more paths on Loughrigg than anywhere else in the Lake District and most of them don't appear on any map. It is therefore essential to take care with route finding.

The Munro's are a list of 282 separate Scottish mountains over 3,000 feet above sea level, originally written by Sir Hugh Munro in 1891. This has become so well known that even people outside hill-walking circles have heard of it and Munro bagging is a popular activity with a certain sort of hairy-kneed walker. In 1992 Alan Dawson published an alternative list of British hills, which instead focussed on relative height, taking as his criterion an elevation of 150m (492 feet) above the surrounding countryside regardless of absolute height. This therefore includes many of the excellent hills of England and ensures that the effort of climbing them will be rewarded with good views. He called them Marilyns (get it). There are about 1,556 Marilyns in the UK, of which Loughrigg Fell is one. Others included in this book are Gummer's How (View 7) and Lingmoor Fell (View 18).

4. Continue up the track through a kissing gate next to a metal gate. After 10 yards fork left and after a further 100 yards fork left again to reach a road junction.

5. Turn left downhill, signed 'Ambleside' for about ¼ mile.

6. Turn left, signed 'Public Bridleway' through a gate signed 'High Close Estate Loughrigg Tarn'. Follow the track between metal fences with

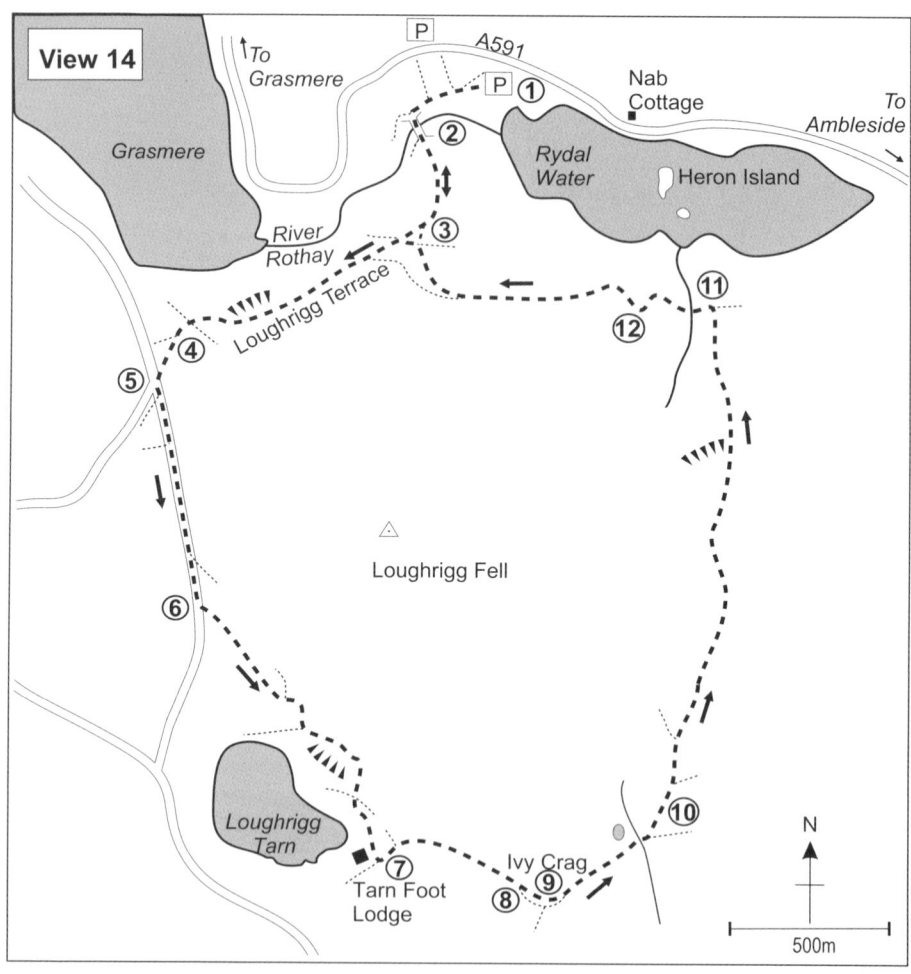

Loughrigg Tarn on the right and views of the Langdale fells beyond. See plate 20, page 58.

Loughrigg Tarn lies at an altitude of 310 feet. It is covered with waterlilies in the summer. It was a favourite spot of the poet Wordsworth and his sister Dorothy and he wrote of it:

"Thus gladdened from our own dear vale we pass
And soon approach Diana's Looking-glass!
To Loughrigg Tarn, round, clear and bright as heaven!"

7. At Tarn Foot Lodge, go through a gate and turn left through another gate on a track signed 'Ambleside'. Climb up, beside a wall on the right, through a gate and continue by the wall.

8. At a fork, where the main path follows the wall, take a small path left up to a bench seat at Ivy Crag. You may, if you wish, avoid scrambling up rocks by taking the right fork alongside the wall and reaching the bench from the far side.

Looking back there is an excellent view of the Langdale Fells with Lingmoor Fell (Walk 18) behind the buildings at Skelwith Bridge. To the right the view is down the length of Windermere.

Ivy Crag

9. From the seat, go ahead to re-join the main path and continue by the wall as more of the length of Windermere comes into view. After the end of the wall on the right continue up the track passing a small tarn on your left and crossing a stream. Continue along the track for 20 yards.

10. Take a minor path forking left. Continue ahead and ignore a right hand fork which only leads back to the track to Ambleside. Stay on the main path, as it climbs to a cairn, ignoring a left fork on a minor path. Now continue ahead downhill as the bulk of Heron Pike and then Rydal Water both come into view. See plate 21, page 59.

The island in front of Nab Cottage is Heron Island.

11. At a track, turn left and follow the track up to a cave.

Rydal Water

The caves are not natural but were once profitable quarries. The slate here lies in beds 10 to 120 feet deep and started life as fine volcanic ash. It was of excellent quality and some had an appealing ripple pattern making it particularly suitable for decorative uses. It was extracted by cutting into the seams rather than opening them up from the surface. The caves are accessible and the upper large one has been used as a concert hall! On the right, the pile of debris is gradually being colonised and from which there is a further view of Rydal Water. For an even more impressive cave you could go to Cathedral Cavern in Little Langdale which is fully described in 'Rainy Days in the Lake District' by Jean Patefield also published by Sigma Press in 2015.

12. Continue on the track to get a view of the north end of Rydal Water with Helm Crag visible above the trees. At a fork ignore a path on the left and take one branching right to go through a gate ahead and down to the outward route. Follow the path to retrace your steps back to the start.

View 15: High Rigg
Stunning views of Blencathra and Skiddaw

High Rigg is in a splendid position rising between the A591 along the Naddle valley and the B5322 along St. John's in the Vale. Hence it is sometimes called Naddle Fell. The walk approaches the fell from the junction of the two valleys, starting with a fairly steep ascent onto a ridge leading to the summit, from where the northern mountains of Blencathra and Skiddaw are seen in all their glory. The route then returns along a good path slightly above St. John's Beck passing an excellent tea garden. The final part of the walk is along a narrow path above a steep bank with the beck below. It is inadvisable to attempt this part of the walk with small children.

What you need to know	
Walking distance	9 km. 5½ miles Height gain: 250 m. 820 feet
Map	OS Explorer OL5 The English Lakes North-eastern area
Starting point	Legburthwaite car park (charge). Grid reference: NY317195
How to get there	Take the A591 Grasmere to Keswick road and north of Thirlmere bear right on the B5322, St. John's in the Vale road towards Threlkeld for ¼ mile to Legburthwaite car park on the left. If travelling by bus, take the 555 service from Lancaster to Keswick to the Stanah Cross stop ¼ mile north of the B5322. You would then start and finish the walk at point 2
Alternative starting points	St. John's in the Vale Church, Grid reference: NY306224, signed from the B5322, where there is a limited amount of parking; from which you would start at point 8 OR you may be able to park on the verge at point 2,

Alternative starting points	Grid reference: NY315194, where you would then both start and finish the walk
Refreshments	Tea garden at Low Bridge End farm

Walk Directions

1. Leave the car park by a small gate in the wall at the far end. Turn left on a track signed 'All walks The dam'.

   On reaching the A591 the road ahead leads over the dam and along the western shore of Thirlmere.

   There were once two small lakes in this valley – Leathers Water and Wythburn Water – together with the villages of Wythburn and Armboth. The area has always been called Thirlmere, which means 'the lake with a gap'. This name was probably given because of the narrow strip of land separating the two lakes. In 1874 Manchester Corporation unveiled plans to flood the valley to supply the expanding city with water. The scheme was strenuously opposed locally and the burgeoning conservation movement formed the Thirlmere Defence Association to contest the parliamentary act that was needed before work could begin. Ultimately, of course, Manchester got its way. Construction began in 1890 and lasted for four years. The dam at the northern end of the valley raised the water level by 54ft and the villages were consigned to history, leaving just Wythburn church.

   The water is carried to Manchester just by gravity and the aqueduct drops by approximately 20 inches per mile along its length. The water flows at walking speed, taking about a day to reach Manchester. At the start of the route there is a tunnel under Dunmail Raise.

   When Thirlmere was created the authorities were very anxious to keep the water pure. All the land that had formerly been used for grazing was cleared of sheep and trees were planted. Public access was discouraged, again in the interests of water purity. Rights of way couldn't be closed, but they weren't well maintained, so people didn't use them much. Nowadays a

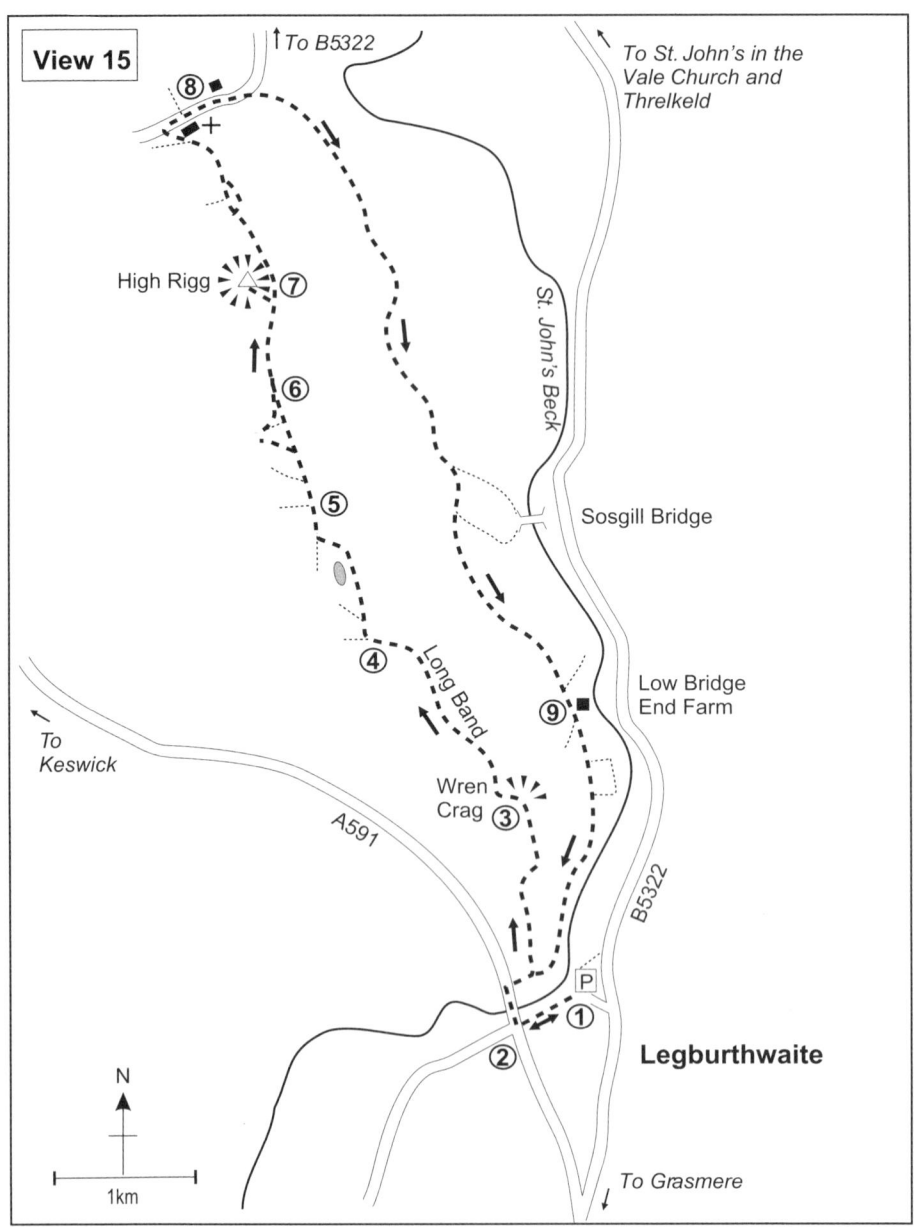

different attitude prevails and visitors are welcomed, together with their car parking fees. A path has been created along the western shore of Thirlmere where formerly you would have been prosecuted for trespassing.

2. Turn right alongside the A591 for 140 yards, with a wall on the right. If you look over the wall you will see St. John's Beck below. Cross a ladder stile on the right by a gate and after 20 yards go uphill to the left of an old oak tree. After a further 50 yards take a path to the left going uphill. The path soon comes out from under trees and climbs steadily up the open fellside. Go down into a dip and then continue up towards Wren Crag ahead.

As you ascend up the rocky path, Thirlmere comes into view with Great How to its left and the steep slopes of Raven Crag to its right. You get an excellent view of the lake from the top of this crag, but to get there is far

Thirlmere and Raven Crag

from being an easy walk. Ahead you look down onto the Vale of St. John with Blencathra beyond. See plate 22, page 59.

3. From Wren Crag, go on down into a dip, through a gap in a wall, and up the other side onto the ridge of Long Band. Go ahead on an undulating path along the heather strewn ridge. Cross a fence at a step stile.

4. Turn right up beside the fence, ignoring a minor path ahead. Just before the top of a rise ignore a small path on the left which, leads to a small hill surmounted with a small cairn from where you can see Bassenthwaite Lake. If you chose to go up this hill return the same way to the fence. Continue by the fence and go gently downhill. After passing a small tarn the path descends more steeply to a ladder stile over a wall.

5. Over the stile, go ahead uphill with a wall on your right. Just before a rocky outcrop ignore a small path branching left and continue up beside the wall. As you approach a seriously boggy area, depending on recent rainfall you may be able to continue ahead beside the wall. If this is not possible keep well to the left and either cross the bog using stepping stones or continue a little bit further where it is easier to cross. At the other side of the bog turn right back towards the wall and as you approach the wall, take a left fork on the main path.

6. Continue with the wall on your right and when the wall turns sharp right continue ahead up to the highest point of High Rigg.

By virtue of the isolated position, the summit dominates the view in all directions. Ahead to the north is an excellent view of Blencathra, also known as Saddleback. To the east is an impressive view of Clough Head. Skiddaw is to the left of Blencathra with the peak of Great Calva visible between the two mountains. To the left of Skiddaw, Bassenthwaite lake is visible; the only lake in the Lake District, as opposed to meres and waters. See plate 23, page 60. To the west is Grisedale Pike and to the left of Catbells we find Red Pike and Robinson. To the south the Helvellyn range is to the left of Thirlmere.

7. The route continues ahead but it is easier to come down from the summit the same way and then take the path below the summit in the direction of the gap between Skiddaw and Blencathra with Tewet Tarn in the foreground. At a fork take the left branch and continue steeply downhill towards a white building. Go through a gate in a wall and down to the left of another building, the Carlisle Diocesan Youth Centre. Turn right along the lane to St. John's in the Vale Church with a convenient seat in the churchyard.

The present building dates from 1845, though there has been a church on the site for much longer. Although located in an isolated spot, the church serves communities in the valleys on both sides of the fell.

St. John's in the Vale Church

8. Turn right out of the churchyard and at a left hand bend take the bridleway on the right signed 'Sosgill Bridge 1¼ miles'. Follow the path by the wall, looking down on the vale and the crags beyond. Keep the wall on the left, ignoring gates on the left from which unmarked and invisible paths go across a field to Sosgill Bridge. Stay on the main path and go through a pedestrian gate where there is a stile about five feet to its right. At a kissing gate, go ahead signed 'Low Bridge End Farm'.

When the ice retreated after the last ice age it scooped out the softer material leaving St. John's vale and the Naddle valley.

9. A path on the left leads down to Low Bridge End tea garden after which you keep left through a gate into a field and continue with another wall on your left. When you reach the beck there are very large boulders strewn about where they have descended from Wren Crag up to the right. Continue through trees above the beck back to the stile onto the A591 and then left back to the start of the walk.

View 16: Black Crag
Outstanding vistas at the heart of the southern Lake District

This is a highly recommended walk at the heart of the southern Lake District with superb views almost every step of the way. The route starts by climbing from Skelwith Bridge using woodland paths and quiet lanes through breathtaking scenery. As you climb the views get better and better until the route reaches the summit of Black Crag with outstanding vistas in every direction. This may sound a formidable challenge but it is not, as the views of mountains and lakes come from Black Crag's position at the heart of the southern fells rather than any very great height. Soon after leaving the summit the route turns north with views of the great peaks of central Lakeland from Coniston Old Man, past the Langdale Pikes with the distant tip of Scafell behind to the Helvellyn range, seen end on. On a really clear day, Blencathra can be glimpsed through the gap of Dunmail Raise. These outstanding views are an immense and satisfying reward for the effort of the climb. The route then descends to Colwith with more enjoyable woodland walking before the final return to Skelwith Bridge.

What you need to know	
Walking distance	9 km. 5½ miles. Height gain: 270 m. 890 feet
Map	OS Explorer OL7 The English Lakes South-eastern area
Starting point	Skelwith Bridge. Grid reference: NY344035
How to get there	Skelwith Bridge lies on the A593, Ambleside Coniston road, about four miles west of Ambleside. At Skelwith Bridge take the B5343 towards Elterwater and Chapel Stile where there is immediately some parking next to the Talbot Arms. If this is full, there is often space to leave a car next to the Community Hall passed at

How to get there cont'd	point 2. The Dungeon Ghyll bus (number 516) from Ambleside also stops at Skelwith Bridge
Alternative starting point	Skelwith Community Hall. Grid reference: NY344031. You would then start at point 2
Refreshments	A tea garden is passed at Elterwater Park Guest House near the end of the walk but this is not always open. Tel: 01539 432414. Refreshments are also available at Skelwith Bridge at the Talbot Arms and Chesters cafe

Walk Directions

1. Return to the junction of the A593 and B5343 and turn right and cross the bridge over the river Brathay. Take the first lane on the left and walk along it as far as the community hall.

2. As the lane bends left at the community hall continue ahead on a track signed 'unsuitable for motors'. When this bends right after 50 yards go ahead on a signed path. Follow this up through a wood, carpeted with bluebells in May, crossing a stream to another lane.

3. Turn left with views opening up over Loughrigg Fell and beyond. At a T-junction turn right signed 'Hawkshead Coniston via Tarns'. At the next junction fork right signed 'Hawkshead' and walk along this lane for about ½ mile as far as a pronounced left hand bend.

4. Continue ahead through a gate on a track signed 'Sunny Brow 1 mile'. (Note: this is not the first gate on the right on a slight left hand bend. It is the second gate on a more obvious bend and the path is, at the time of writing, signed.) Follow the track uphill, going through a further gate across the track, as far as a metal gate on the left at the top of a rise.

5. Some 20 yards after the gate on the left, bear right on a smaller path and climb up through a European larch plantation. Cross a fence leaving the plantation and bear right, uphill, with views appearing over Windermere to the right and behind to Esthwaite Water. The path (eventually) turns back

left continuing uphill. It then turns right and left again to reach a ladder stile over a wall. Do not be deceived by the well-constructed large stone cairn ahead. This is not the top. Keep on past it to the trig point, complete with National Trust plaque identifying Black Crag, on the summit.

From the summit, looking first to the east is Windermere. Then turning right you see Blelham Tarn, Esthwaite Water, Tarn Hows and Coniston Water all laid out at your feet with, on a clear day, glimpses of the sparkling sea beyond. See plate 24, page 60.

6. After admiring the view from the summit, go ahead over a ladder stile for about 150 yards along the ridge for the view of Lingmoor Fell (View 18) and the fells beyond. See plate 25, page 61. Return to the trig point. Facing the large cairn you passed on the way up, take a path leading right towards

The approach to Black Crag

Tarn Hows and Coniston Water beyond. The path soon becomes quite clear and is marked by cairns. Follow it down to a track by a gate.

7. Turn right and follow the track downhill. Ignore a track on the left through a gate and continue beside a wall on your left. Go past a farm on a track to the left and then ahead along a track through a gap in the wall.

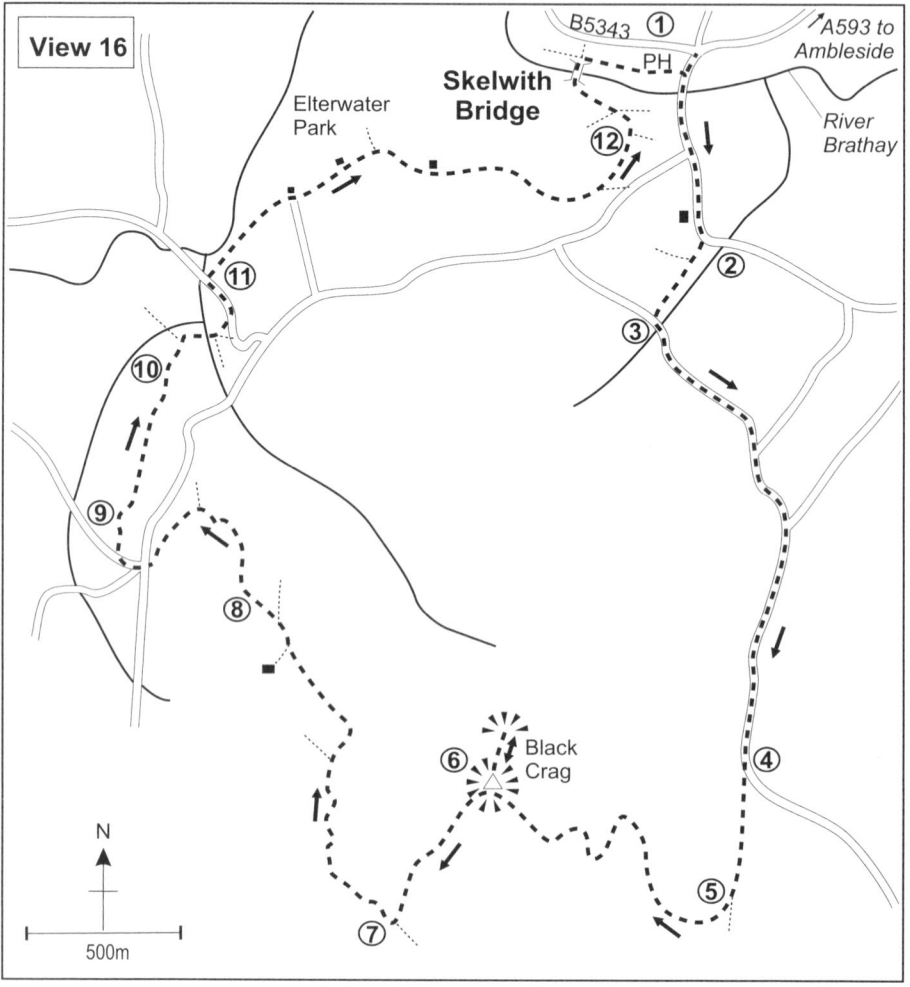

The views ahead of the central fells are still magnificent from this lower elevation. As you go downhill there is a glimpse of another lake, Elterwater.

8. Some 100 yards after passing the farm the path reaches a fork; bear left on a signed footpath. Stay close to a wall on the left down to a gate in a field corner and then continue down with the wall now on the right. Shortly after some bends, ignore a path through a gate on the right, and continue along the main path up and then down to arrive at a major road. Cross the road and keep ahead on a tiny lane. Bear right at a fork after 50 yards, signed 'Hall Park Hallgarth' for a further 50 yards.

9. Turn right through a field gate on a public bridleway signed 'Colwith ¾ mile', through woodland to reach a T-junction in front of a gate in a wall.

Skelwith Force

10. Turn right to find a footbridge over a stream (not the footbridge to the left). Over the bridge bear left and follow a walled path, ignoring paths uphill on the right, to a lane. Turn left for 125 yards.

11. Turn right through a gated squeeze-stile, signed 'Skelwith Bridge 1 mile'. Follow the path steeply uphill, made easier by steps, and then across a field. Keep ahead to the right of a bungalow then across a drive. Continue past a guest house 'Elterwater Park' where, at the time of writing, there is a tea garden which opens more in the summer months. Carry on along the clear track and pass to the right of Park Cottage. When the track forks in clear sight of a road bear left for 200 yards to a kissing gate into woodland and continue for 120 yards to a finger post.

12. Go ahead signed ' Elterwater 1½ Coniston 8¼ Skelwith avoiding A593'. Cross a footbridge over the river Brathay and then turn right signed 'Skelwith Bridge'. Pass Skelwith Force on your right and continue between buildings back to where this walk started.

The footbridge over the river Brathay commemorates Trevor Woodburn, a local man who proposed the route in 1998. It was officially opened in July 2007. Kirkstone Quarries Ltd. operated from the buildings that you pass. Stone was finished here until 2012.

View 17: Oxford and Arnison Crags
Two crags with views of Ullswater from the south

South of Patterdale, between Grisedale and Deepdale, are routes up Fairfield. This short but fairly steep walk also ascends from Patterdale at the southern tip of Ullswater. Alfred Wainwright says that Arnison Crag is "often visited for the fine view it offers of the head of Ullswater" and it is "a low hill with a summit worthy of a mountain". The walk takes in Oxford Crag, from where there are excellent views of Ullswater, and then continues up to Arnison Crag for somewhat better views in all directions. You may return the same way, but the full circular walk continues down through Glenamara Park.

What you need to know	
Walking distance	4½ km. 3 miles Height gain: 290 m. 950 feet
Map	OS Explorer OL5 The English Lakes North-eastern area
Starting point	Patterdale Hotel car park (charge). Grid reference: NY395159
How to get there	Patterdale is on the A592 Windermere Penrith road at the southern end of Ullswater. The car park is on the opposite side of the road to the hotel. Patterdale is also served by the seasonal 508 bus from Windermere to Penrith and the seasonal 208 bus from Keswick
Refreshments	The Place Fell Inn at the Patterdale Hotel serves bar meals and has a good selection of draught ales

Walk Directions

1. Take the signed public footpath to the right of the hotel. Behind the hotel, turn left in front of a wooden building (do not go ahead through gates).

Follow the signed public footpath into woodland, initially with a small stream on your right. Cross the stream and go ahead through a kissing gate onto the open fell. At the start of a rocky section, ignore a very small path on the right leading to a gate. Continue uphill with glimpses of Ullswater to the right, to reach a wooden field gate and kissing gate on the right and a tall wall ahead.

Through the gate is the return route. The deer wall borders Glenamara Park which this walk visits on the return. It deters the most agile of deer from escaping the park.

2. Do not go through the gate but go uphill with the tall deer wall on your right. As you climb gently beside the wall the magnificent view unfolds over the southern reaches of Ullswater. The path gets somewhat steeper as you ascend between the wall and Oxford Crag on your left. Go up onto the crag.

From Oxford Crag you cannot see the full length of Ullswater as it bends to the right out of sight near Gowbarrow Fell (View 19) on its left. However, you do have an excellent view of Place Fell beyond Patterdale on the right of the lake.

3. Continue ahead by the wall as the path ascends more steeply. As you approach Arnison Crag the path deviates left from the wall. After about 50 yards ignore a small path climbing steeply to the left. Instead go ahead for 100 yards and take an easier route on the left up onto Arnison Crag with a small cairn marking the summit.

There is a full 360° view not only of the lake (see plate 26, page 61) but of the higher fells by which Arnison Crag is surrounded. To the left of Gowbarrow Fell you can see Sheffield Pike and turning to the left there is the Helvellyn range. To the south-west rise the peaks of St. Sunday Crag and Fairfield. Also High Street is to the south-east.

4. From the summit return down the way you came up and now turn left at the T-junction regaining the previous route. After 30 yards, fork right and

take the path contouring round the hillside with the deer wall down on the right. Follow the path as it approaches the wall and then goes up beside it. It then goes down, now with a wire fence on top of the wall as an even greater deterrent to the deer, and then deviates from the wall to descend gently into a valley.

Going left up the valley is a route up St. Sunday Crag and on to Fairfield.

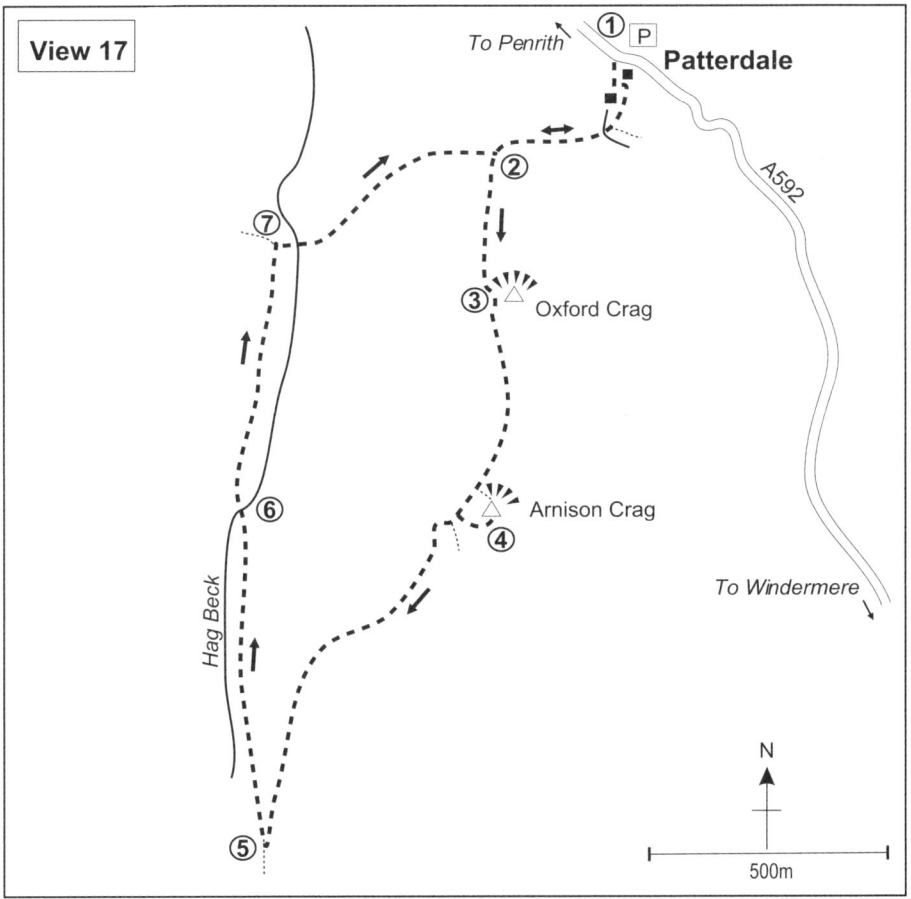

5. Turn sharp right down the valley back towards the wall. Cross the wall at a ladder stile into Glenamara Park. Continue down the valley beside Hag Beck.

The building directly ahead is Patterdale Hall which has had a long history. John Mounsey, 'King of Patterdale', lived there. His main claim to fame was when he led a party of dales men to Stybarrow Crag when Scottish marauders were expected. He deployed his troops, then left them saying, "I'm a bit lame lads. I'm gan yam (going home)." It is now an adventure learning centre owned by Bolton School.

Just before reaching a wood note a young rowan tree growing in a precarious position at the top of a rock in the beck.

A precarious Rowan

6. Cross Hag Beck and continue downhill now with the beck on your right. The path deviates to the left away from the beck and becomes increasingly obscure. Keep to the right of most of the trees and about 100 yards above the beck as you go downhill to a major track. If you lose the path entirely just continue downhill to the track.

7. Turn right along the track for about 80 yards to cross Hag Beck by stepping stones. Continue ahead to reach the wooden field gate and kissing gate passed at point 2 near the start of this walk. Through the gate turn left down to the gate into the wood and back to Patterdale.

View 18: Lingmoor Fell
Magnificent views of the Langdales

Brown How, the highest crag of Lingmoor Fell, is the best place to see the fells in the Great Langdale district. It comprises a number of rocky outcrops and there are exceptional views of such classics as the Langdale Pikes, Bowfell, the Coniston Fells and many more. Though by no means the longest walk in this book, this must be a serious contender for the Most Strenuous Walk. It climbs Lingmoor Fell from Blea Tarn with plenty of opportunity to stand and stare at the magnificent views of the Langdales. The route continues along a ridge with a view of Blea Tarn and then past Side Pike, an impressive crag.

What you need to know	
Walking distance	5 km. 3 miles Height gain: 290 m. 950 feet
Map	OS Explorer OL6 The English Lakes South-western area
Starting point	Blea Tarn car park. Grid reference: NY295043
How to get there	From the A593, take the B5343 Great Langdale road. At the head of the valley, take the minor road left for 1½ miles. Just after Blea Tarn on the right there is a National Trust car park on the left (charge for non-members)
Refreshments	None on the route. The Old Dungeon Ghyll is in Great Langdale and The Three Shires Inn is in Little Langdale

Walk Directions

1. From the car park, turn right along the road for 300 yards.

2. Watch for a wall on the left coming up from the tarn to join the wall along the left side of the road. After a further 20 yards take an unsigned, lightly

trodden but still visible, path on the right up the fellside heading towards trees. If you miss this path continue along the road to take a path on the right just before Bleatarn House to rejoin the route at point 3.

The ascent of Lingmoor gives the best views of Blea Tarn and it was this view that inspired Wordsworth to write in 'The Excursion':

> *Behold! Beneath our feet a little lowly Vale*
> *A lowly Vale, and yet uplifted high*
> *Among the mountains ...*

3. Turn right at a cross-path towards the edge of a steep tree lined valley to continue uphill, essentially along the right hand side of this valley. The path goes through a gap in the wall and continues up steeply, bending

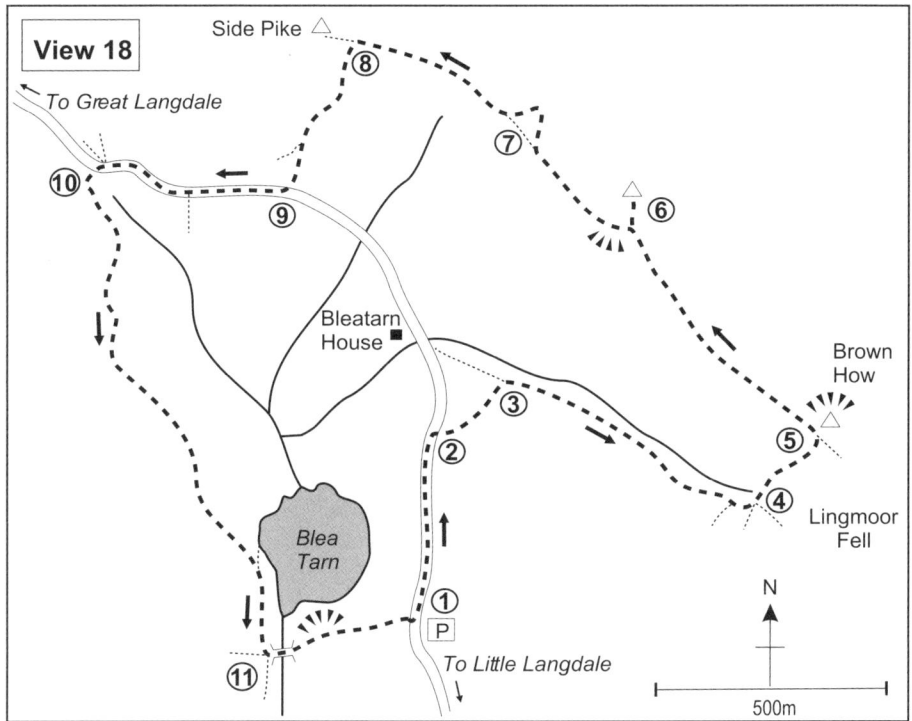

right away from the tree lined valley and then back towards the valley. When you can see a wall ahead ignore a small path to the right and follow the path down to the left to a stile over the wall.

4. Over the stile, turn left still uphill with the wall and then a fence on the left. Near the top, you may avoid a rock strewn section by detouring right on a grassy path and then on to a crossing fence. Go over the stile to the summit cairn.

Lingmoor Fell is a Marilyn, a relatively isolated fell with no neighbouring peaks to block the view. For more information about Marilyns see View 14. The summit is one of several rocky outcrops forming Lingmoor Fell each of which has its own name: this is Brown How. It is a rocky outcrop superimposed with a large cairn. Lingmoor Fell gives unparalleled views of the great mountains all around since it is the dividing range between Great and Little Langdale. 'Ling' is an old norse word for heather and it is from this plant which grows freely round the summit, especially on the northern side, that the fell gets its name. It has been much quarried, as have some of the surrounding hills, for its fine green slate and evidence of this past and present industry is seen all around.

The path to the south, in the direction of Windermere, goes along Lingmoor Fell and down into the Little Langdale valley, passing Busk Pike. The position of Brown How, overlooking the head of the Great Langdale valley, provides unrivalled views of the high Lakeland mountains. To the north you look down into Great Langdale and the Langdale Pikes rising above the head of the valley. To the left the superlative view takes in Green Gable, Great Gable, Bowfell and Crinkle Crags. See plate 27, page 62.

5. From the summit, head along the ridge in a north-westerly direction towards the Langdale Pikes with a broken down wall and fence on your left. Squeeze between the fence and another rocky outcrop. At the start of a boggy area, take the path going a little way away from the fence. This path returns to the fence. When the wall and fence bend sharply left go ahead to a small crag with a small cairn for the view down to the Old Dungeon Ghyll and the Langdale Pikes.

There is also an excellent view of Blea Tarn from here.

6. It is now easiest to return to the fence corner and follow the fence downhill. Turn right, along the path with the now unbroken wall on the left. At the top of a steep descent, zig-zag to the right to reach a stile at a wall corner.

7. Over the stile, follow the path to the right in the direction of the rocky peak of Side Pike, to a kissing gate.

    The path ahead leads round to the left of Side Pike and through a narrow gap between rocks called a 'Fat Man's Agony' and then up to the summit for more superb, but similar views of the Langdale Pikes.

Looking down to Blea Tarn

8. Do not go through the kissing gate but turn left downhill with a fence on your right. Do not cross a stile on your right but continue down to the road.

9. At the road you may wish to turn left back to the car park, but for a fairly gentle finish to this demanding walk, going around Blea Tarn, turn right for 400 yards ignoring a public footpath on the left, which goes through boggy land.

10. Over a cattle grid, turn left for 30 yards and then left on a track signed 'Wrynose Pass 1¼ mile'. Follow this to a gate into the woods at the side of Blea Tarn and then alongside the tarn.

It is very difficult to appreciate that the wild country we see is as much a man-made landscape as any city. One of the places where research has been done into this is Blea Tarn. Pollen grains are very slow to rot down so by looking at the pollen grains trapped in sediment at the bottom of the tarn we can tell quite a lot about the vegetation around the tarn at different times in the past. Until about 3000 BC the area was thickly forested. Neolithic people started the process of cutting down the trees. The counts of elm pollen fall dramatically and it is thought they used elm leaves and young shoots as bedding and fodder for animals. In the silt at the bottom of the tarn is a layer showing that the removal of the trees led to increased erosion from the denuded hillsides. Down the centuries this process continued until the hills were left bare of trees and it is only in the last century that the process of deforrestation has been slightly reversed.

11. Shortly after passing the end of the tarn, turn left over a footbridge and go along the southern end of the tarn for a final view of the Langdale Pikes and Side Pike (See plate 28, page 62) before reaching the car park.

You may turn left out of the car park and return to the A593 via Little Langdale. You will then pass the Three Shires Inn which gets its name from the three shires stone on Wrynose pass where the old counties of Lancashire, Westmorland and Cumberland met. The coat of arms of the inn has the emblems of these counties.

View 19: Gowbarrow Fell and Ullswater
The most beautiful lake

This walk combines all the elements that make the Lake District so special. It starts at one of the Lakes best known beauty spots Aira Force waterfall. And goes up the tree-clad gorge carved out by Aira Beck. Two spectacular waterfalls Aira Force and High Force and more cascades are passed before going onto Gowbarrow Fell for a view of the mountains and Ullswater. Ullswater is a serious contender for the Most Beautiful Lake and this walk gives the best view of it from part of the way along the lake.

What you need to know	
Walking distance	7 km. 4½ miles Height gain: 330 m. 1100 feet
Map	OS Explorer OL5 The English Lakes North-eastern area
Starting point	Aira Force National Trust car park (charge for non-members). Grid reference NY400200
How to get there	Aira Force is on the A592 Patterdale Penrith road just over 100 yards east of the junction with the A5091. The seasonal 508 bus from Windermere to Penrith and the seasonal 208 bus from Keswick to Patterdale both serve Aira Force
Alternative starting points	If the Aira Force car park is full, there are two National Trust car parks (both charge) on the A5091. The southern one is Park Brow and the other is High Cascades. Paths lead down to Aira Beck from both of these
Refreshments	Aira Force tea room has tables outside overlooking Ullswater. It is signed from the car park near the entrance

Aria Force

Walk Directions

1. Walk to the rear of the car park and take the path to the right of the National Trust information kiosk. Follow the main path and go through a gate.

   The Greystoke family who owned the area in the nineteenth century followed the fashion for romantic landscaping and they planted 60,000 trees of both native and introduced species around the falls. This area is called the Pinetum and is a collection of conifers.

2. Just past money trees on the left, turn left and follow the clear path past another money tree.

   Go past paths on the left and right (the one on the right leads down to a bridge from where there is the classic view of Aira Force). Continue up to the top of the lower fall.

   The first money trees passed are stumps of felled trees and the last one passed is a fallen beech about 10 yards long. These show that money really does grow on trees at Aira Force. People have hammered thousands of coins into the wood, presumably as an atavistic offering to the gods of this special place.

3. Cross the river (Aira Beck) by the footbridge at the top of the fall. Over the bridge turn left and after 25 yards ignore a path going up steps to the right. Continue along the river bank until the path goes right, up a mainly stepped path to a T-junction with another path.

   Aira Force may not be the highest waterfall in the Lake District or carry the greatest volume of water but it is certainly the best known and is visited by crowds of people every year. This is undoubtedly due to the charm of the falls' setting. It has been a popular beauty spot for over two hundred years and featured in many eighteenth century guide books and guides used to lead people up to admire the scene. Legends were 'borrowed' to add to the romance. It was said that a crusader met Emma, the daughter of a local lord, by the falls. While he was away she pined and started walking in her sleep.

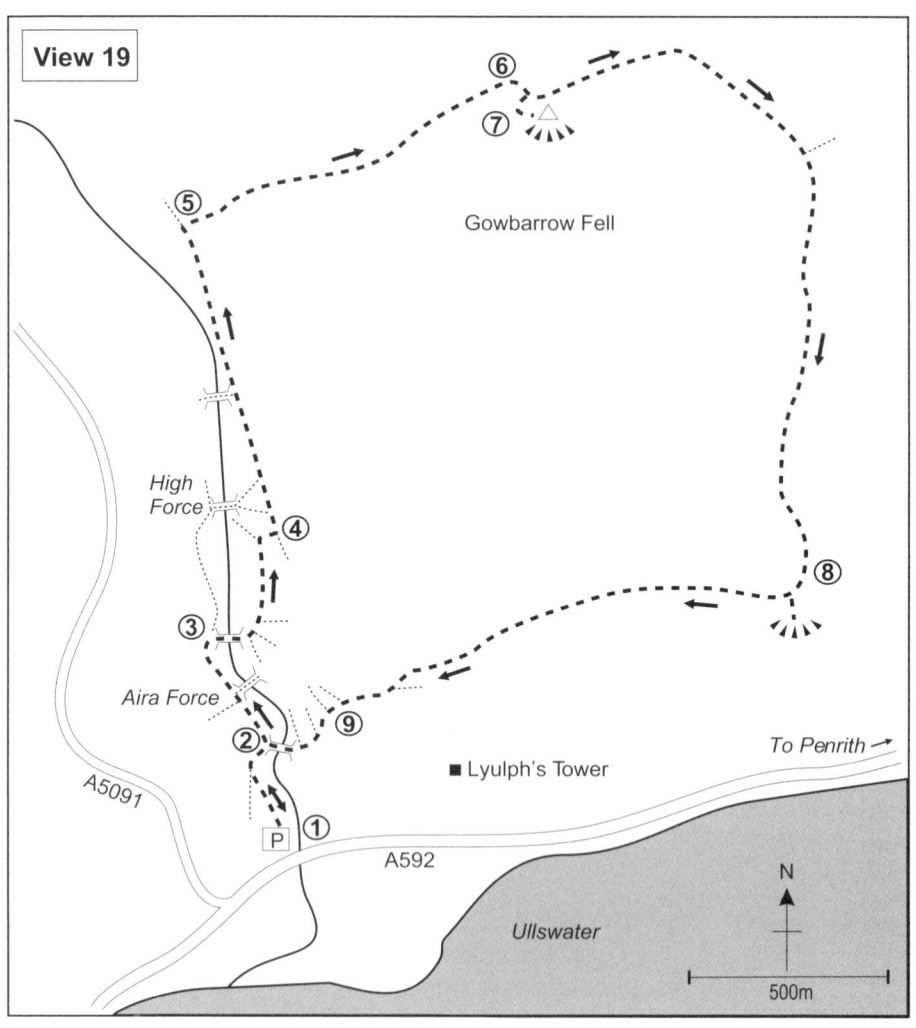

One night he returned and his call woke her. She fell into the torrent and was drowned. The crusader spent the rest of his life, so the story goes, roaming round the falls mourning her and living as a hermit in a cave. Wordsworth used the story and the setting as the theme for his poem 'The Somnambulist'.

4. Turn left to continue on this path past a stony path leading down to the upper falls. Follow the river passing more falls to your left. Ignore a path on your left going over a footbridge and up to High Cascades car park. Go ahead signed 'Gowbarrow' and through a wooden gate onto the open fell.

5. Just before a wooden field gate, turn right on a path signed 'Aira Crag Gowbarrow Summit'. This reaches a stile in a wall after 90 yards and then continues uphill with a wall on the left.

As you climb there are superb views backwards (every excuse to stop and admire them) of the foot of Ullswater and High Street. Helvellyn gradually comes into view.

Gowbarrow is often called Gowbarrow Park, which refers to the fact that it was a medieval deer park. These were created by the feudal overlords to

Gowbarrow Fell Summit

protect their hunting. In 1906 Gowbarrow Park, including the famous waterfalls, came on the market as housing plots. The National Trust launched an appeal and £12,000 was raised to buy the 750 acres and save it for the nation.

6. Near the highest point of the path by the wall, bear right and head for the trig point on Gowbarrow Fell. As you approach the summit take the path going right and then left to the top.

   The view of the fells is glorious: to the south, Place Fell with High Street beyond and Helvellyn to its right. See plate 29, page 63. To the north-west are Blencathra and Skiddaw and to the north-east the Pennines. You can still look forward to the highlight of the walk with the views over Ullswater still to come.

7. After admiring the view leave the summit by the same path round the right and left bends and now take the path ahead down below the summit and head towards a wall corner seen below and slightly left. Before the wall the path bends right to contour round the hillside and is joined by a path coming in from the left. Continue on this path round the hillside and be surprised as more and more of Ullswater comes into view. After a series of bends there is a gate on the left giving access to a cairn.

   The view is outstanding with most of the lake visible and also the fells to the south. See plate 30, page 63. Ullswater claims to be the most beautiful lake in England with Derwent Water (View 20) also a serious contender.

   Ullswater is the second largest lake in the Lake District and is 7½ miles long. The geology of the surrounding area is very varied. It was formed by three glaciers, which accounts for its serpentine shape and the variety of scenery surrounding it. The craggy landscape at the head of the lake – the throat of Patterdale – where steep fells crowd round the lake are on hard volcanic rock resistant to erosion. In the middle are the softer Skiddaw slates and at the foot is the rolling countryside of sandstone and limestone.

On the shore of Ullswater, beneath Gowbarrow Fell, Dorothy Wordsworth saw the daffodils that were later immortalised by her brother William. She wrote in her diary 'they seemed as if they verily laughed with the wind'.

Having admired it from above, enjoy it from a different angle by taking a trip on one of the steamers that ply the lake. The full trip round the lake takes well over two hours but if time is more limited, you can just enjoy the short excursion from Glenridding or Pooley Bridge to Howtown. In a 2017, addition to the round the lake service, the first and last boats of the day call at Aira Force. For details of the timetable telephone 017684 82229 or visit **www.ullswater-steamers.co.uk**

8. Return to the path and continue round the hillside passing a seat from which the view to the south is just as impressive. The path gradually

Aira Beck

descends and as it steepens you can see Lyulph's Tower to the left as more of the lake is visible.

Lyulph's Tower was built in 1794 as a hunting lodge on the site of an earlier defensive pele tower and is privately owned by the Howard family. Lyulph is said to have come from the name of a Viking called L'Ulf who may also have given his name to Ullswater.

9. Go through a gate into woodland and follow the path down to a footbridge over the river. Go up steps on the other side and then bear left back to the car park.

View 20: Walla Crag and Friar's Crag
One walk, three special viewpoints

Starting at the Theatre by the Lake in Keswick there is a steady climb, up to the first viewpoint at Castlehead. This is followed by a stiffer climb onto Walla Crag, from where there are exceptional views over Derwent Water with its artistically arranged scattering of islands, frequently called the Jewel of the Lake District; with good reason. There is then a gentle descent to Ashness Bridge, a contender for the most photographed packhorse bridge in the Lake District due to its location and stunning views. The walk finishes along the lakeshore to Friar's Crag, famous for the view down Derwent Water.

Derwent Water Jetties

What you need to know	
Walking distance	10 km. 6½ miles Height gain: 350 m. 1150 feet
Map	OS Explorer OL4 The English Lakes North-western area
Starting point	The Theatre by the Lake, Keswick. Grid reference: NY264228
How to get there	From Keswick Town Centre take the B5289 Borrowdale road and follow the road sign to the Lakeside car park (charge). The Theatre by the Lake is at the far end of the car park
Alternative starting points	Great Wood National Trust car park (free to members). Grid reference NY271214. Take a path signed 'To the lake 300m 5mins' onto the car park entrance road and across the Borrowdale road and down six steps. At a T-junction turn left signed 'To the lake 150m 2mins' and pick up the walk at point 13, OR with a bit of ingenuity about 600 feet of ascent may be avoided by utilising the 555 bus from Keswick towards Kendal and alighting at the Castlerigg stop at High Nest, (grid reference NY287227) on the A591 at the brow of a hill, about two miles from Keswick Bus station. Then take the signed path south-west to a lane where you turn left to join the route at point 6; this misses out on the Castlehead viewpoint and shortens the walk by almost two miles
Refreshments	The Café by the Lake is between the theatre and Derwent Water. It has spectacular views across the lake to Cat Bells and beyond. There is also a tea room at Springs Farm, passed during point 4, which serves home-made cakes, scones and sandwiches

Walk Directions

1. From the theatre go down to the lakeshore. Ignore the first two paths on the left both going up steps and take the third path on the left signed

'Cockshot Wood' to walk, initially with an open field on the right for 100 yards, and then going into a wood. At a junction continue ahead signed 'Castlehead Viewpoint'. At the far side of the wood go ahead, slightly left, on a hedged path still signed 'Castlehead Viewpoint'.

2. Go up steps and across the Borrowdale road and up three more steps. Turn left. Ignore the first path on right after 20 yards. After a further 35 yards turn right by a seat and a plaque. Join a path and go uphill along the left-hand side of the wood.

The plaque commemorates Sir John Scurrah Randles, a member of the executive of the National Trust, who gifted Castlehead, Cockshot Wood and Crow Park to the nation.

3. At the end of the field on the left, turn right still signed 'Castlehead Viewpoint' with a toposcope pointing out Castle Crag (View 13) at the far end of Derwent Water, and Cat Bells and Red Pike across the lake. These peaks are seen from a higher elevation at Walla Crag. Return to point 3 and now turn right. After 10 yards fork left downhill to go out of the wood at a kissing gate and follow the path towards houses.

4. At the road turn right and at the end of the road pass Springs Farm and Tea Room, a good place for a coffee break or even lunch, if you did not set off too early. Continue on the public footpath signed 'Rakefoot/Castlerigg', through a gate and into Springs Wood. Follow the path up beside Brockle Beck.

5. After 300 yards, turn right signed 'Rakefoot Farm Walla Crag Castlerigg stone circle'. This is where the path ahead used to cross the beck by a footbridge washed away during storm Desmond in December 2015. Follow the path uphill, still with the beck tumbling down on your left, as the view over Derwent Water unfolds. At a finger post, where the path to the right leads to Great Wood, continue ahead signed 'Castlerigg $1/5$ mile Walla Crag 1 mile'. Cross a footbridge over the beck and follow the path up to a lane.

6. Turn right and then bear right for 100 yards where a track forks left to a farm.

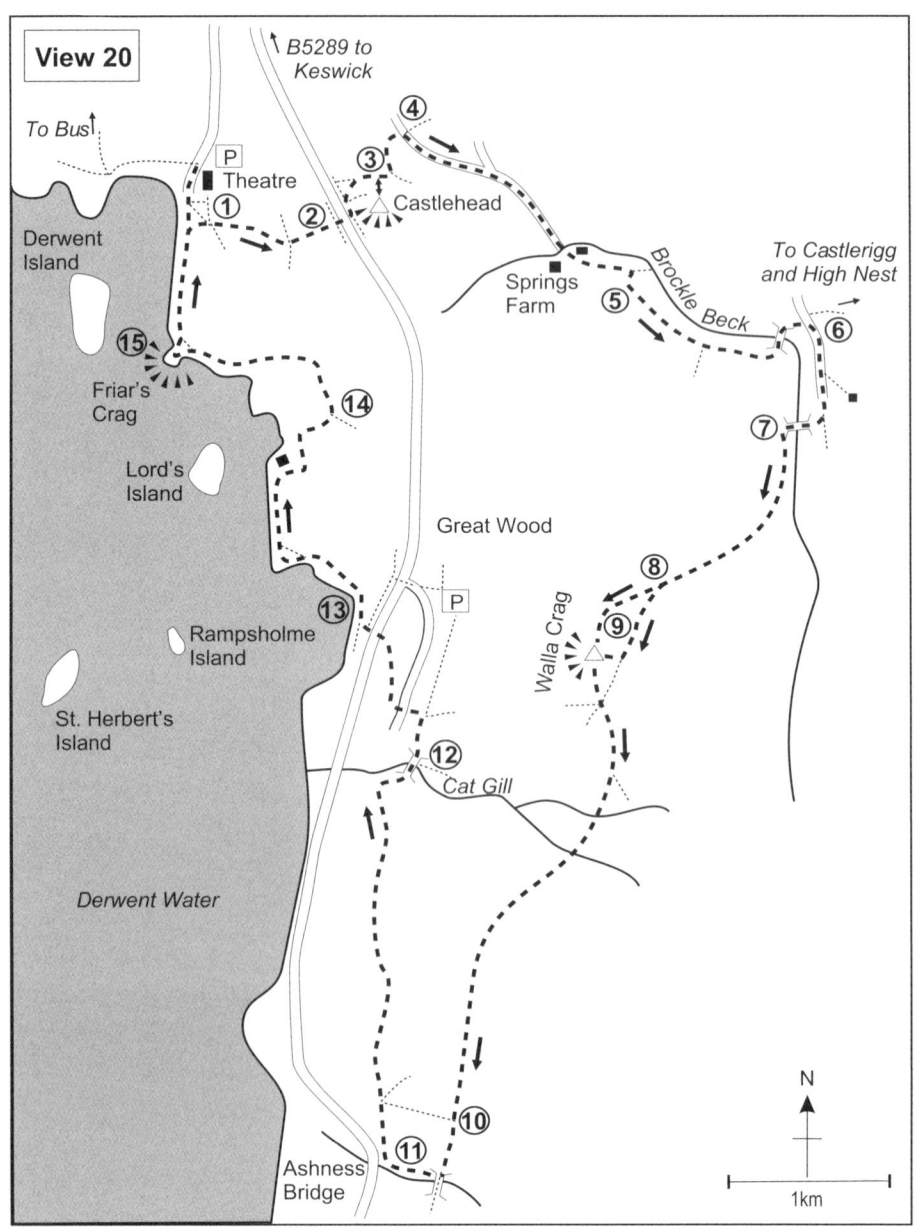

7. Cross a footbridge on the right over Brockle Beck and follow the footpath signed 'Walla Crag' with a wall on the right and then through a wooden gate, keeping alongside the wall. The view behind and to your right takes in Bassenthwaite Lake, Skiddaw and Blencathra.

8. At a large cairn, the path through a kissing gate on the right cannot be described as easy. It has stunning views but is rocky and precipitous in places. To avoid this take the easier way up by continuing alongside the wall to a stile on the right. Over the stile, go ahead to a small cairn. Both routes take you to the highest point over Walla Crag.

To the right the view takes in Derwent Water and Bassenthwaite Lake with the hills of Galloway beyond. After the last ice age Derwent Water and Bassenthwaite Lake formed one lake. Silt, carried down by rivers gradually separated them. The view of Derwent Water (see plate 31, page 64) with its many islands and the mountains beyond is even better than that seen earlier from Castlehead.

9. With your back to the lake leave the summit heading downhill to your right into the top of Lady's Rake, where another stile re-crosses the wall. Lady's Rake is a narrow cleft in the face of Walla Crag. Over the stile, turn right for 15 yards. At a cairn take the track to the left that heads across the moorland, rather than the one to your right that heads very steeply downhill into Cat Gill. At a fork, where the left branch heads up towards the prominent peak of Bleaberry Fell, take the right branch gently downhill. Cross tributaries of Cat Gill plunging down to the right.

As you go along the path there are views into the Jaws of Borrowdale at the head of Derwent Water, including Kings How, Castle Crag (View 13) and the high fells. The marshlands, where the river Derwent is depositing material into the lake is a bird's-foot delta; like the Mississippi, but on a very much smaller scale.

10. Go through a gate in a wall and then turn right in front of the next gate signed 'Ashness Bridge 150 m 5 mins'.

Ashness Bridge is an ancient packhorse bridge on the lane from Borrowdale up to Watendlath, the home of Judith Paris in Hugh Walpole's Rogue Herries chronicles. The lane takes you down to the B5289 Borrowdale road which is served by the number 78 bus. At Ashness Gate you could also finish this excursion back to Keswick by launch on Derwent Water; for timetables see **www.keswick-launch.co.uk**

Ashness Bridge

11. Turn right on the lane and 20 yards from the bridge take a path on the right signed 'Great Wood 1¼ miles 55 mins'. Go through a gate in a wall and then bear left signed 'Great Wood 1 mile 50 mins'. The path eventually goes into woodland and then up beside a wall to cross Cat Gill at a footbridge.

12. Continue ahead signed 'Derwent Water ½ mile 20 mins'. Just after a wooden barrier, turn left on a path going downhill. (The path ahead goes

to Great Wood car park.) Cross the exit road from the car park and go ahead on a path to emerge on the Borrowdale road at a bus stop. Cross the road and go ahead to the lake.

13. At the lake turn right and follow the shore path. After passing to the right of a house the track crosses a cattle grid.

    Derwent Water has four permanent islands: Derwent, Lord's, Rampsholme and St. Herbert's. It also is said to have a floating island which sometimes appears towards the end of summer and consists of vegetable matter that rises to the surface on a cushion of methane gas.

14. At a finger post, go left signed 'Friar's Crag ½ mile 15mins Keswick 1¼ miles 40mins'. The path returns to the lakeshore and then reaches a gate into a wood. After 15 yards, turn left up steps to reach the third and last viewpoint at Friar's Crag. See plate 32, page 64.

    Friar's Crag is renowned as the most favoured view in the Lake District. It looks straight down into the Jaws of Borrowdale with Castle Crag in the middle. It is easily accessible from Keswick so you are unlikely to have it to yourself. It is so named as it is said to be the launch point for monks making a pilgrimage to St. Herbert's Island. It was given to the National Trust in 1920 as a memorial to Canon Raunsley, one of the three founders of the National Trust.

15. From Friar's Crag take the path with the lake to the left and return to the theatre.

    For a scenic route to the bus station go through a gate opposite the theatre into Crow Park and follow the path with the lake on your left. When the path ends keep in the same direction and through a gate into woodland on your left. Through the gate take the gravel path to a T-junction. Turn right on the track for 60 yards passing laid-up boats and then right again on a major track. This leads out of the wood in the direction of Skiddaw. Continue on a road to the bus station by Booths supermarket.

Also from Sigma Leisure:

Rainy Days in the Lake District
Jean Patefield

The Lake District's picturesque patchwork of lakes, valleys, woodlands and mountains make it one of the premier places in Britain to enjoy the great outdoors. Choose the wrong week and experiencing the great outdoors can be more of an endurance test than a pleasure. Rainy Days in the Lakes offers a solution to this problem with over twenty suggestions of free and interesting things to do in the Lake District in less than perfect weather. Each expedition is designed to take half a day and suggestions are made for combining them together to make an enjoyable and cheap wet day out with a break for lunch in the dry.
£8.99

All of our books are all available online at **www.sigmapress.co.uk** or through booksellers. For a free catalogue, please contact:

**SIGMA LEISURE, STOBART HOUSE, PONTYCLERC,
PENYBANC ROAD
AMMANFORD, CARMARTHENSHIRE SA18 3HP
Tel: 01269 593100**

info@sigmapress.co.uk   www.sigmapress.co.uk